COMPLETE

ATHLETE

...

WOMEN'S
SOCCER

2017

Copyright© 2017, Complete Athlete, LLC

Front cover photo: Madison Jabara

ISBN-978-0-692-79698-6

The purchase of this book entitles the buyer to reproduce student activity pages for single classroom use only. Other use requires written permission of publisher. All rights reserved.

Printed in the United States of America.

At the time of this book's publication, all facts and figures cited are the most current available. All telephone numbers, addresses, and website URLs are accurate and active. All publications, organizations, websites, and other resources exist as described in the book, and all have been verified. The authors and Publisher/Complete Athlete, LLC make no warranty or guarantee concerning the information and materials given out by organizations or content found at websites, and we are not responsible for any changes that occur after this book's publication. If you find an error, please contact Complete Athlete, LLC.

Complete Athlete, LLC
660 Newport Center Drive
Suite 200
Newport Beach, CA 92660
Phone: (714) 949-3845
www.mycompleteathlete.com

*To every young woman aspiring to be a **Complete Athlete** in every aspect of your life—this book is for you.*

TABLE OF CONTENTS

INTRODUCTION

DO YOU DREAM OF BECOMING THE NEXT MIA HAMM? CARLI LLOYD? ALEX MORGAN?

What could be better than playing a game you love and making money at it?

The idea of becoming a professional athlete and getting paid to play is very exciting. But the truth is, only a very small number of athletes make it to the pros. About 1 in 16,000 high school athletes becomes a professional athlete. According to the U.S. Department of Education, fewer than 1 out of every 100 high school athletes receives a scholarship of any kind to a Division I school.

BUT THAT DOESN'T MEAN YOU SHOULD GIVE UP ON YOUR DREAM.

If you're determined to become a professional soccer player, or even to earn a college scholarship, this book can help show you the way.

This book will help you prepare to play soccer at the highest levels AND be a desirable recruit for college and/or professional coaches. It emphasizes the concept that success is not just dependent on one's natural ability; it is also influenced by attitude and behavior, as well as how you treat yourself and others, both on and off the field of play. Guidelines, suggestions, and real-life examples are provided by our team of experts, whom you can read about at the end of this book.

A youth athlete who is determined to earn a college scholarship and/or to become a professional soccer player needs to become a **COMPLETE ATHLETE**. There are five levels to becoming a **COMPLETE ATHLETE**. Generally speaking, the five levels correspond to the following (although there may be some overlap):

Level 1 - Elementary school athlete
Level 2 - Middle school athlete
Level 3 - High school athlete
Level 4 - College athlete
Level 5 - Professional athlete

A **COMPLETE ATHLETE** must also achieve the highest levels in five different categories:

ATTITUDE refers to how you behave on the field. For instance, listening quietly while the coach is talking and showing respect for your fellow players both demonstrate that you have a good attitude.

PREPARATION refers to off-the-field activities, such as keeping your uniform clean and equipment well maintained, learning everything you can about your sport, practicing, and more.

FITNESS refers to the physical fitness needed to compete in your sport.

TECHNIQUE revolves around skill level, including mastering the basics and specializing in a particular position.

LIFESTYLE refers to how you treat yourself, including eating right and getting enough sleep. It also includes getting good grades and being a good member of your family and your community.

THE COMPLETE ATHLETE MATRIX

ATTITUDE
- Respect
- Sportsmanship
- Teamwork
- Professionalism
- Leadership

PREPARATION
- Practice
- Nutrition
- Hydration
- Recovery
- Mentality

FITNESS
- Lower-Body Strength
- Upper-Body Strength
- Flexibility/Mobility
- Core Strength
- Speed/Quickness/ Endurance

TECHNIQUE
- Foundational Ball Skills/Dribbling
- Passing
- Ball Control
- Ball-Striking/Shooting
- Heading

LIFESTYLE
- Family
- Academics
- Social Life
- Role Model
- Living Your Sport

Each of the pillars that helps hold up a category is part of the overall development and character of a **COMPLETE ATHLETE**. "Character," according to Merriam-Webster, is "the way someone thinks, feels, and behaves." All of these aspects influence what kind of a person and player you are.

If you look at the matrix above, you'll see that several categories have attributes that relate to your actions off the field. What you do off the field affects how you play on the field. For instance, maintaining good fitness will make a big difference in your ability to perform the techniques needed to play soccer.

The key here is that just because someone is a professional player in the sense of being paid to play, he or she might not necessarily be considered a professional according to this system.

The next few sections of this book will discuss what you need to know, do, and be at each succeeding level in order to become a **COMPLETE ATHLETE**.

You have more power than you think.

True, this can be difficult to believe sometimes—especially during those sometimes-trying preteen and teenage years, when your daughter seems determined to question or challenge everything you say. But if you ever start to doubt how much influence you still have over your child, just pay attention the next time she makes a big play or a huge mistake in a game. Where is the very first place she looks?

Chances are, it is to wherever you are sitting.

And chances are, you are reacting to what just happened.

And chances are, whether you are cheering, grimacing, clapping, shouting, looking proud, looking embarrassed, or looking angry—that is going to color the way your daughter plays for the rest of the game, how she reacts to the win or loss, how she feels on the drive home, how she views the entire sport, and even how she views herself.

We all want the best for our children, and we all want our children to be the best at whatever they do. But what is best for one child may not be what is best for another. *Complete Athlete* is a guide to managing expectations, whether your daughter is a standout player or part of the supporting cast. Often, our children can accomplish more than we imagined them capable of; other times, they are far more fragile than we suspect. How are you reacting to each victory and each disappointment? As you explore each level, think seriously about what your role is in developing your daughter into something more than just a great soccer player. What are you teaching her about responsibility when you make a consistent effort to get her to practice on time? What are you teaching her about respect with the way you speak to and about her coaches, teammates, and their families? What will you say to her about resilience when she faces defeat, or humility when she wins big? How are these lessons she will carry with her beyond the soccer field, and into life?

Sometimes, the right answer is obvious. Sometimes, you may not have the foggiest idea as to what you should say. That is where the *Complete Athlete* can help. By laying out clear guidelines with regards to the appropriate skills, game knowledge, health and nutritional demands, and personal and emotional maturity for each level, you can access tips, examples, ideas, and real-life applications both in the book and via the app. This is an interactive, multifaceted, in-the-moment approach to investing in our children's career and character.

At each stage of her career—whether she is just starting out or looking to go pro—you will be your daughter's most important and influential fan. You will always be the person who loves your daughter most of all, and vice-versa. More than her coaches, more than her teammates, how you chose to act and model your behavior will lay the groundwork for who your daughter becomes.

You have more power than you think.

Sincerely,
Walid Khoury and Ziad Khoury

DEAR ATHLETE,

You have big dreams and a lot of drive. Do you know how we know this? Simply the fact that you have picked up this book and are reading it tells us that you are a young woman who wants to do more than just the minimum; you are someone who wants to develop her skills and potential. Already, you are demonstrating one of the most important aspects of making that dream become a reality. Someone who is willing to learn and is open to coaching will always be more successful than someone who thinks she already knows it all. Always.

Complete Athlete is designed to help guide you through your career as you grow as both an athlete and a person. It will emphasize three key areas—lifestyle, preparation, and attitude—each of which is an essential part of developing and maximizing your talent.

Before we begin, however, it might be helpful to consider how each of these areas contributes to your overall character and to ask yourself some questions:

Lifestyle means your consistent commitment to making good choices. Are you eating healthy foods? Are you sleeping as much as you should? Are you as focused on your schoolwork as you are on your athletic training? Are you avoiding illegal drugs and alcohol? Are you keeping your body and mind in top shape by maintaining a healthy body image based on what is best for your body-type—not what social pressure says you should look like? Are you spending time with positive people and in healthy relationships that won't get you into trouble? If the answer is "no" to any of these questions, are you ready to make the necessary changes ... today?

Preparation is your willingness to do the necessary work required to be ready every time you step onto the soccer field. It requires dedication to learning rules and practicing drills so that you have the fundamentals down-pat. It also means that you arrive at practice or games with your equipment clean and organized, and with your head in the right place so that you are ready to learn and ready to give every minute of practice your fullest and best attention. Do you have what it takes to do all the necessary "homework" to grow in every area— even when that preparation isn't fun?

Attitude has to do with your maturity both in terms of how you treat others as well as yourself. Respect for your parents, coaches, and teammates is a huge part of what makes you an appealing recruit for elite teams. It doesn't matter how good a player is; if she refuses to listen to instruction, talks back, or is someone who stirs up trouble between other players, no coach is going to want her on the team. An athlete who is willing to work hard, eager to learn, and easy to get along with is going to be a leader and standout player—no matter where she falls on the roster. Your attitude matters because it is the main way that people see how you interact with the world and how you value yourself. Can you be confident without being arrogant? Can you handle disappointment without beating yourself up? How will you react if you don't make the shot, or don't get invited to join the team, or don't receive the scholarship offer? How will you react if you do? The way you handle yourself in these situations matters a great deal.

If you are serious about your career as a soccer player, you need to own the journey and you need to own it now. Your parents and coaches are an essential part of reaching your goals but, ultimately, it all comes down to whether or not you are willing to put in the time and effort to become the person you need to become in order to succeed. No one else can do it for you. You must have the integrity to consistently make the right decisions about how you live, how you prepare, and about your attitude—when every eye in the stadium is glued to you, and when no one at all is looking. That is how you

become more than just a soccer player. That is how you become a **COMPLETE ATHLETE**.

Sincerely,
Walid Khoury and Ziad Khoury

DEAR COACHES,

The name of this book, *Complete Athlete*, is no accident. Although your primary responsibility is to grow the young women under your care into top-notch soccer players, you also play an important role in helping them mature as whole, complete people. Whether you are a seasoned professional or a parent volunteering in the role, a good coach does so much more than just teach game skills.

As you read this book and review the accompanying apps, we hope that you will consider how they can complement your job both on and off the field. How can these tips and suggestions help you interact with players and their families in more meaningful and impactful ways? For example, it is important for coaches to communicate clearly with parents about what they should reasonably expect their child to learn each season or at each level. This book provides a clear set of guidelines to outline those points and help the entire unit of the team—players, coaches, and families—to operate in a healthy and mutually supportive manner. You all want the same thing: to see each and every athlete reach her fullest potential.

At the same time that you are teaching your athletes the fundamentals and finer points of the game, you are also teaching them about the fundamentals and finer points of being a good citizen and a responsible individual. Your attitude and example show your players the importance of being a good teammate and the satisfaction that comes with self-reliance. The way you talk about and interact with parents, game officials, other coaches—even the waitress at the restaurant where you all go out together after a game—models for the girls what respect, appreciation, and basic manners look like.

Please don't let these opportunities slip through your hands or become lost in the noise of competition. It is easy for coaches to fall into the habit of making the game about themselves, rather than their players. Wins and losses can become personal—a reflection on you and your abilities—rather than teaching opportunities for your players. Every practice, every game, every single interaction is a chance to influence these young women.

A good coach prepares his or her players for the game; a great coach prepares them for life! We are excited to walk alongside you as you train, push, encourage, discipline, cheer for, cry with, nurture, educate, comfort, counsel, mentor, and celebrate every member of your team. Thank you for your commitment to coaching, and thank you for your dedication to these special young people. Together, we can help them to maximize their opportunities and become more than just good players. Together, we can inspire them to become a **COMPLETE ATHLETE**.

Sincerely,
Walid Khoury and Ziad Khoury

IN LEVEL 1

a soccer player learns what she needs to know at a beginner level. She also begins to lay the foundation for achieving success at high levels of play. Even if you've already been playing soccer for a while, you should make sure you understand what is expected at this level. You should also make sure that you meet all of the criteria in each category discussed in the chapter.

1.1 ATTITUDE

A **POSITIVE ATTITUDE** is essential to an athlete's success both on and off the playing field, especially as she moves into higher levels of play. In fact, college coaches seek out athletes who display positive attitudes.

A positive attitude is something that can be developed with practice, just like any other skill. A **COMPLETE ATHLETE** makes a habit of demonstrating the following five attributes:

RESPECT

SPORTSMANSHIP

TEAMWORK

PROFESSIONALISM

LEADERSHIP

ATHLETES » At half-time, your attitude has to be positive. Just because you missed a goal or allowed the other team to score or missed a tackle or messed up in any way, you can't come into the team huddle at half-time and hang your head or sulk while the coach is talking. You're not just hurting yourself, you're putting yourself in a position to fail. You're hurting your teammates because they see how you are behaving and, if you're a leader, your conduct brings them down, too. The focus of half-time should not be you—it should be what your team needs to do in the second half.

COACHES » The first thing a coach should do at half-time after a rough start to the game is to calm the team down. The emphasis should never be on the failures and disappointments, because this can get the players angry with one another. Make sure that the focus is always on having a positive attitude and clear sense of the game plan going forward; if you don't do that, or if you allow one player to mope, it is going to affect the whole team and the team is not going to recover.

KASSI MCCLUSKIE » *It's great for parents to encourage their children to try something new and to stick it out for a little bit while they get used to it, before deciding if they want to quit and try something else instead or not. But sometimes, parents can push their children into an activity where the child has no interest or natural ability, all because the parent wants to live vicariously through the child. I would encourage parents to periodically check with their children to gauge their attitude toward the sport and to see if their heart is really in it or if they might be better suited to try something else.*

When I was in elementary school, my mom was worried that my dad might have been pushing me too hard to be an athlete because my dad had been a star hockey player until an injury killed his professional chances. Dad said he was just pushing me because he wanted me to be the best I could be, but he didn't want to keep doing it if I wasn't enjoying soccer. He decided to try to figure out if I was truly playing for myself by asking me, "Hey, since this is all so expensive, if we couldn't afford it, what would you do instead? Would you stop playing soccer? Would you decide to do something else?" I answered, "You can't take my dream away." And my dad said later that he was so happy to know, then, that his daughter really was playing for herself and not out of a sense of obligation to anyone else.

RESPECT

RESPECT means treating others in ways that show they have worth and value, and being considerate of other people's feelings. At Level 1, youth soccer players should always treat their coaches with respect. These are the people who have taken time out of their busy lives to pass on their love for and knowledge of soccer, and to provide opportunities for players to learn more about the game and to play well. For those same reasons, they should treat all game officials with respect as well.

HOW TO DEMONSTRATE RESPECT
FOR YOUR COACHES »

- When you arrive at a game or practice, greet your coach politely.
- Find out how your coach prefers to be addressed,

whether by his or her first name, by Mr. or Mrs.
_____, or simply as Coach. Always address your
coach the way he or she prefers to be addressed.
- Listen carefully and don't fidget when your coaches
are speaking.
- When your coaches are speaking directly to you,
look them in the eye and don't interrupt.
- Don't talk back or sass your coaches or
game officials.
- Follow directions without complaining; in other
words, do what you're told to do.

ATHLETES » One of the greatest teams I ever coached
had a level of respect that was just exceptional. The
moment they left their cars in the parking lot, they always came to find me. They showed up early to practice
to help me set up. They always started with, "Hello,
Coach! How are you doing? How's your day?" Even at a
very young age—most of these girls weren't even in high
school yet—this particular group of young ladies had an
incredible sense of respect.

And it wasn't just for me; they carried that respect, onto
the sidelines and the field, toward one another. It was
amazing to watch them during practice; when someone
made a mistake or passed the ball to the wrong player,
the girls always stayed positive and encouraged one
another: "No problem! Keep working hard!"

After practice was done, they stayed and lent a hand
packing up, helping me take my gear to the car and never
leaving—every single one of them—without saying,
"Have a great day, Coach! Thank you." That was one
of the most important things for me to see. Those girls

weren't just there for the big moments; they were really invested in every aspect of how the team operated. Setting up and taking down aren't really the exciting or glamorous parts of playing a sport, but they all pitched in because they saw what needed to be done and they understood why it mattered.

That is something I will always take with me from that team. As young as they were, the respect they showed to me as a coach and to each other was remarkable and really made our time together a joy. *–Walid*

PARENTS >> Attitude starts while you're in the car on the way to practice or a game. Before you even get to the field, your child is either preparing to get the most out of what is coming or she is not. We see this a lot with younger players, especially. If they have an argument with their parents, they usually get out of the car pouting or angry, and that affects the place where their mind is, which in turn affects the way they play that day. However, when an athlete climbs out of the car and is smiling and positive and ready to focus on the task at hand, they usually have great practices.

COACHES >> Sometimes you have to single out individuals at half-time to help them erase whatever mistakes from the first half they are still replaying.

I remember in one of the games, we had a penalty kick late in the first half. One of the top players stepped up to take it—and she missed it. The referee whistled the end of the half, and then we were immediately in our half-time break, trying to talk to the team about what we should be doing in the second half. All the players were focused on what I was saying, except for the girl who had just missed the shot. Her head was down, her shoulders were slumped—you could just see her entire demeanor was shut down and she wasn't hearing a word we were saying. After I finished talking to the whole team, I went to her individually and said, "Hey, look me in the eyes. Look me in the eyes." She lifted her head up and I could see how upset she was, but I told her, "You've got to put it behind you and we've got to move on. The most important play in the game is the next play. You've got to respect the game and this is part of the game. This is simply one of the ups and downs of the game."

I'll never forget when she looked me in the eyes and saw that I was focused only on her and didn't value her less as a player or as a person, and that I still needed her to perform her part for the team. She took a deep breath and was able to put everything behind her and ended up being one of the biggest impact players with how she stepped up in the second half and helped us win the game. It was a significant moment in reminding me of the importance of helping each player get her head right in the middle of a game. How the team works together matters, but each member needs that individualized attention sometimes, too. *–Walid*

COMPLETE ATHLETE

JOIN THE CONVERSATION!
Download the Complete Athlete app now!

SPORTSMANSHIP

Good **SPORTSMANSHIP** starts with respect for one's teammates, opponents, coaches, and officials. It also includes playing with integrity. Playing with integrity means following the rules and never cheating.

At Level 1, a youth soccer player should be familiar enough with the basic rules of the game to always play by those rules. [To review basic rules, go to Appendix 1.] She should never try to bend the rules or cheat. In addition, she should always abide by what the coaches and officials say in terms of penalties and not argue with them. After all, they know more than she does when it comes to what's fair and what's not in the game of soccer.

PARENTS >> Respect for referees and coaches is essential and at these younger ages in Level 1, it really starts with the parents.

You can see the behavior at any youth soccer game. Who are parents attacking the most? All you hear is, "Oh, referee, that was a foul, that was offside, that was... ." Whatever it is, there are always parents yelling at the ref that it was a bad call. The players hear their parents complaining about everything, and they start imitating their parents and showing disrespect for the referees.

Here's the thing: As the game goes on and the ref has had just about enough of everybody yelling at him or her, if there is a call that could go one way or another, the ref is going to give it to the team whose parents and players have shown him or her the most respect.

It's no different than going to school. Parents don't come into school and yell at the teacher because that would model to their children that a teacher is not someone worthy of respect. The same thing should be true on the soccer field. The parents have got to set the example by sitting down and supporting whatever the referee decision is and by being positive with their kids. The players need to understand that the referee is no different than a teacher or a policeman or anybody who's an authority figure; they should treat him or her with the utmost respect. If you disagree with something, you let your coach know; you don't throw a fit yourself.

As a parent, that must be a pillar for your behavior at games, starting at the lowest level. If you demonstrate respect for referees and coaches, that is a practice that will become a habit for your child as she develops as an athlete. If you are always complaining about every call, always complaining if things don't go your way, always yelling that the ref is clueless, then your child is going to believe that is what she should be doing as well. Those habits are going to stay with her for a lifetime.

But if you model from the beginning respect for the referee, respect for coaches, respect for teammates, those are tremendous habits to have, and they'll follow your child the rest of her life and give her a great reputation. Reputations can follow you. Referees talk to each other and they can give each other the heads-up on a team or a player. They say, "This is the kid with the attitude," or "That team has irrational parents." Beyond the importance of raising a child who shows appropriate respect, there is simply the fact that a bad reputation can mean iffy calls don't go your way. Consider both the big and small picture when you are tempted to yell at a ref!

COACHES >> One of the greatest things you can teach athletes is sportsmanship. At a very young age, it is important that athletes learn that sportsmanship is a huge part of competition. After every game, you need to teach players to go over immediately and shake hands with the opposing team, no matter the outcome of the game. This needs to become second nature so that players do it automatically: show respect for every single player on the other side, walking to the referees and shaking their hands and thanking them for refereeing the game, too. This is so important to stress with your athletes.

A few years ago when I was coaching my U-10 team, the outcome of the championship game didn't go the way we wanted—we lost in a heartbreaker in the last five minutes of the game. When the referee blew the final whistle, everyone's head was just hanging. That is when one of our team leaders stepped up and took the initiative to gather everyone into a circle and to tell them they had all played well; then she told her teammates to keep their heads up and congratulate the other team for winning. It was just so amazing, as a coach, to watch a young person immediately spring into action and rally her team to show good sportsmanship. She had learned that at an early age so that it was second nature. That is so refreshing to see, because it will take an athlete a long, long way in her career. *–Ziad*

TEAMWORK

TEAMWORK means working together as a group in order to achieve a goal. In sports, players contribute their individual skills and efforts in cooperation with their teammates to win games.

At Level 1, youth soccer players learn what it means to play as part of a team and not just as an individual athlete, a skill that is important at every level of play. To pass Level 1, a youth soccer player must always share the ball with other players and never hog the ball during games. She also must cooperate with coaching plans that allow everyone to participate no matter their skill level.

PROFESSIONALISM

Certainly a youth soccer player is not a **PROFESSIONAL** in the sense of being paid to play. However, developing the attitude and behaviors of a professional can help her move up more easily through the levels.

Professionals in many fields require some kind of proper attire and appearance. For example, most lawyers wear suits. Many doctors wear white coats. At Level 1, a youth soccer player should always arrive on time with all her equipment at hand. She should also have a neat and clean appearance, including a uniform that has been recently washed and shoes that are properly tied.

COACHES » Teamwork is so important and it is something we have to encourage in our children from day one, because it doesn't always come naturally to kids. Especially at the younger ages, there always seems to be one player whose skills are a bit ahead and she can dribble around everybody. In a game, whenever she gets the ball, she doesn't pass it—she just runs with it, scores, and does the same thing the next time her feet touch the ball. Sometimes she misses, but every time she gets the ball she just keeps going the whole way. At half-time, I have to remind her to use her teammates. The best example I have to illustrate the point to the kids is to pick up a pencil or stick and show them how easily it breaks by itself. If I put three together, it is much harder to break them. If I bundle eleven together, it is impossible. I have each child try to break it and they see how strong the sticks are together. I explain to them that is what will happen if we play as a team—we will be so much harder to break.

It's not a bad idea to remind parents of this, either, since they are often the ones on the sidelines yelling at their daughter to run with the ball. Of course we want the points for our side, but if that one-star player gets tired or hurt and no one else has had a chance to handle the ball in a game situation, what then? We are all proud of our kids and want them to shine, but it is essential that they learn how to work with one another so that the whole team can achieve even greater success by combining their talents. —*Walid*

KASSI MCCLUSKIE >> *One of the most important things I learned in my playing career was when my coach told us there were five core values, and if we all demonstrated them as a team, we would be successful. They were hard work, teamwork, concentration, discipline, and preparation. We had to memorize those five things and read things our coach had for us on each characteristic. She explained the significance of each one on our personal and our team performance, and made sure that we had at least a basic understanding of each concept.*

I was very young when those ideas were first introduced,

and I don't think I really appreciated them at the time. But I had internalized the idea that hard work was an ingredient to success, that teamwork was an essential element in a strong group, that if I paid attention to what I was learning and had self-discipline, ate right, got enough sleep, and practiced what I needed to—this would all contribute to my overall success. My understanding grew as I did, and now I can see how those five values have played a part not only in every team of which I've been a part, from middle school through college, but also in every project I've attempted, every interview I've ever done, and every job I've ever held.

LEADERSHIP

A good leader is able to inspire and motivate others to do things they would not normally do, or to perform better than they would on their own. Developing leadership skills can benefit a youth athlete not only in high school and college but in their professional lives as well.

At Level 1, a youth soccer player is not expected to take on a leadership role. However, by watching how her coaches inspire and motivate the team, she can begin to develop an understanding of what traits an effective leader has—and what traits an ineffective leader has.

COACHES >> One of the things I do as a coach, especially for the younger ages around 7 to 10, is that I choose a different captain for every game. I explain that to them at the beginning of the season, and it helps teach all the players how to become leaders and to take responsibility. I explain that the captain's job is to represent the team, to be positive on the field, to lead the team, and to speak on the team's behalf. It is great to see the players working so hard to be the one picked for the next game. Some coaches choose just one player for the whole season but, at that age, I really believe it is more important to help each child learn how to become a leader. We mold them by putting them in that position and giving them that chance. –*Walid*

CAMILLE LEVIN ➤➤ *It is up to you, as a player, to be coachable. You need to be confident in what you are doing and how you play, but at the same time be open to hearing other opinions and flexible when the team needs it. I played every position on the field in youth, high school, and even in college. I think that experience made me more valuable to my team, more interesting to recruiters, and more sure of myself as an athlete. But first, I had to be willing to change positions from what I was used to, and that required me to listen to my coaches and be willing to do what the team asked of me.*

Keep in mind that if your coach is moving you, it is for one of two reasons: Either it is necessary so that the best 11 players can be on the field, or it's because there is a certain situation where the coach believes your skills are going to help boost the team. Don't let a change get into your head; instead of getting upset about it, embrace it! Your coach believes in your talent enough to try you in a new position.

1.2 PREPARATION

PREPARATION refers to off-the-field activities, such as practicing skills, eating right, staying hydrated, getting enough rest, and mentally preparing for a practice and games. Coaches love athletes who prepare: These are the players who are eager to learn, eager to play, and, ultimately, eager to win. They are the athletes that coaches want to help succeed, because they already have a winning attitude. Preparation also helps athletes feel positive and confident in their ability to perform.

A **COMPLETE ATHLETE** prepares to perform on the field of play by continuously improving on the following:

PRACTICE

NUTRITION

HYDRATION

RECOVERY

MENTALITY

PRACTICE

At Level 1, soccer should revolve around having fun, getting exercise, and learning to be part of a team. Nevertheless, **PRACTICE** is essential for becoming skilled at the techniques of the sport. Practicing also helps a youth athlete avoid injuries and become a better, more confident player.

Team practices usually occur several times per week. They are run by the team coaches, who plan the activities based on the techniques they believe the team needs to work on. Individual practice is performed by a youth athlete outside of regularly scheduled team practice sessions, without the coach and team present.

HOW MUCH TIME TO PRACTICE »

There is little agreement on the exact amount of time a youth athlete should practice on his or her own. Most experts agree that it's better to be fully engaged in practice for a shorter period of time, rather than mindlessly performing the same technique over and over again. In other words, the type of practice is more important than the amount of time spent practicing. When a youth athlete is able to do the same skill over and over again consistently, he or she has mastered that skill.

HOW TO PRACTICE »

- Create a practice schedule that includes the skills you need to improve as well as those you already do well.
- Ask your coaches to provide suggestions for which skills should be practiced.

- Work on the same skills the coaches emphasize during team practices.
- Concentrate on each activity performed during practice.

SAMPLE PRACTICE SESSION >>

- Warm up and stretch
- Drill 1
- Drill 2
- Drill 3
- Cool down and stretch

NOTE >> It is common for youth athletes to feel frustrated or want to quit while trying to master a technique. Not only does improvement come with regular practice, but youth athletes will also learn to overcome adversity to achieve goals, a skill that will help them in all areas of life.

PARENTS >> At this level, kids are usually practicing twice a week or once a week, and the coach is there giving them instructions the whole time. That is great for building fundamentals, but if parents want to do some work on their own, try varying up the techniques. If you come up with creative games to practice skills, you can keep the fun and joy in the game at this stage, rather than making it seem like a chore.

One game to try is to practice juggling the ball, trying to beat one another's records back and forth. Another is just to have a shoot-out, trying to see who can make the most shots out of ten. Another game that we absolutely love is "soccer tennis." You can start this as early as age 7 and keep playing it through as a professional. Go to a tennis court and let the ball bounce before playing it, and pass it back and forth. When you get to the higher levels, try it with only one bounce or without any bounces at all. But at Level 1, if you let the ball bounce unlimited times while you play it and then pass it back over, you can have a whole lot of fun while still practicing footwork. It creates a bond and gives you extra time with your child.

Don't make it about "Here's how you need to cut," or "No, you missed this shot—how could you? Let's do 20 more so you can hit that." It is too early at this stage. What you want to foster is love of the game, so allow your child to have fun when she is doing her extra practices—and create some fun memories together, too!

NUTRITION

NUTRITION plays a key role in athletic performance. Youth athletes are building muscle, burning calories, and growing. They need to eat and drink regularly to make up for the loss of calories they are burning and the fluids they are using during practice and actual games.

An active youth soccer player needs to consume healthy food and beverages in order to:

- Replenish her energy supply
- Maintain hydration
- Obtain the vitamins and minerals needed to support metabolism, tissue growth, and repair
- Prevent injuries and/or illnesses
- Perform at her best both on and off the field

NOTE >> All of the *Complete Athlete* sports nutrition guidelines were provided by Courtney M. Sullivan, founder of Nutrition for Body and Mind. Sullivan is a Registered Dietitian certified by the Academy of Nutrition and Dietetics, and a Certified Personal Trainer recognized by the National Academy of Sports Medicine. Appendix 2 provides more detailed guidelines as well as suggested meals and recipes developed by Sullivan.

GENERAL SPORTS NUTRITION GUIDELINES >>

- All athletes should consume 5 or more balanced meals spread throughout the day, every 3–4 hours.
- Meals should be eaten 2–3 hours before practice or games, and snacks eaten 1-1 $\frac{1}{2}$ hours before practice or games.
- Eat when you're hungry to prevent lean-muscle breakdown; stop when you're full to prevent being sluggish.
- Eat breakfast within 30 minutes of waking up to prevent lean-muscle breakdown, increase energy and concentration, and maintain good blood-sugar control. Choose whole grains, fresh fruit, and lean protein for breakfast.
- Eat well-balanced meals and snacks, consisting of carbohydrates, lean proteins, and heart-healthy fats. Drink a protein shake or eat a snack or meal that has equal amounts of protein and carbohydrates within 30 minutes after a workout.
- Choose fresh, whole foods when possible (instead of processed foods that are packaged or refined) to increase nutritional value. Avoid foods that are high in sugar and/or trans fats.

LEVEL-1 ATHLETE NUTRITION GUIDELINES >>

Each individual has different macronutrient needs, based on height, weight, age, activity level, and genetic background. The following macronutrient guidelines are based on age and estimated activity level for a Level-1 athlete:

- 60% carbohydrate
- 15% protein
- 25% fat
- No more than 7% saturated fat
- No trans fat
- 25 grams of fiber per day
- No more than 150 calories per day from sugar (37.5 grams or 9 teaspoons)

To fulfill the macronutrient needs listed above, choose from the following:

CARBOHYDRATES High fiber foods, such as whole-grain bread, brown rice, whole-grain pasta (or gluten-free versions), beans, starchy vegetables (e.g., corn, peas, potatoes), quinoa, and cereal

PROTEINS Chicken, turkey, or fish, especially wild salmon, tuna, trout, mackerel, and sardines, which are high in heart-healthy omega-3 fatty acids

FATS Low-fat cheese, nuts/nut butters (natural peanut butter or almond butter), avocado, seeds, and heart-healthy oils like extra-virgin olive oil, canola oil, grape-seed oil, and flaxseed oil

VEGETABLES Preferably leafy green vegetables

PARENTS » In tournaments, teams may have two games in a day with lunch in between. Parents will often take the kids to the closest place to eat, which is usually some kind of fast food. When they come back for the second game, they can barely even run—and it's not because they are tired or sore from the first game; it's because they are weighed down by greasy, trashy food!

You, as the parent, are the one who is driving them at this age, so you are the one who ultimately has the power to decide where you point the car. You are in charge, so you need to be willing to make healthy choices; pack a healthy lunch or go to Subway. Bring Gatorade and healthy snacks for between games for your child to eat right after their first game so they are ready to play the next one. It's very important. You are investing a whole day; your kid is going to be there a whole day. Be prepared. Nutrition for an athlete is fuel for a car. It doesn't matter how good the car is—if it doesn't have gas in it, you can't drive it. We want to establish good habits as young as possible so that the children will follow through when they get older. –*Walid*

HYDRATION

All athletes need to drink water before, during, and after practices and games. This is especially important on days when both temperatures and humidity levels are high. If a youth soccer player does not drink enough water, she could suffer from dehydration. Warning signs of dehydration include:

- Thirst
- Irritability
- Headache
- Weakness
- Dizziness
- Cramps
- Nausea
- Increased risk of injury

HOW TO MAINTAIN PROPER HYDRATION* >>

- Before exercise, drink 16-20 full ounces within the 2-hour period prior to exercise.
- During exercise, drink 4-6 full ounces.
- After exercise, replace 24 full ounces for every one pound of body weight lost during exercise.
- * Adapted from guidelines provided by the American College of Sports Medicine (ACSM)

PARENTS >> Even at these early stages, hydration is so important, because players this young can still face injury or cramping if they do not have the proper level. Leading into a big event and especially in certain times of the year when the weather plays a huge factor with heat and dryness, athletes have to be proactive about staying hydrated and, at this level, parents are in charge of this. You have to make sure your child is drinking plenty of water leading into game weekend, regardless of the weather. Keep an eye on the forecast, though, because if it is going to be hot and dry, you will need to up your child's water intake even more.

The State Cup happens in June in Southern California, and one year, it was going to be 98 degrees on game day. On Tuesday, I told the players to be sure they drank a lot of water ahead of time, but on Saturday, we had a player pass out during the game. The referee stopped play, and we brought her to the bench to get water in her and check her out. I asked what happened and she said, "I don't know. I was thirsty, I started getting a headache, then I started feeling weak and dizzy." I asked her if she had drunk a lot of water leading up to the game; she said she drank a lot ... right before the game.

Children can't always understand the big picture of how the body works and how hydration is a key factor days out from the actual game. That is why parents need to make sure they are monitoring their child's water intake before any big event. –*Walid*

**COMPLETE
ATHLETE**

JOIN THE CONVERSATION!
Download the Complete Athlete app now!

RECOVERY

Youth soccer players need to eat and drink within 30 minutes of a practice or game to make up for the calories they are burning and fluids they are using. Replenishing calories and fluids also aids in muscle recovery and repair.

HOW TO REPLENISH CALORIES AND FLUIDS >>

- Drink 24 ounces of fluid for every pound of sweat lost within a 2-hour period of a game or practice.
- Consume 5-10 grams of protein plus an equal amount of carbohydrates within the 30-minute recovery window.

SLEEP Just as increased activity creates a greater need for calories, it also creates a greater need for sleep. **RECOVERY** also means allowing the body to rest and heal from the demands of practices and games.

According to the National Sleep Foundation, a Level-1 youth athlete should get 10-11 hours of sleep each night for proper growth and development. If that's not possible, or if a youth soccer player needs additional recovery time, she can take short naps (no longer than 30 minutes) or engage in quiet rest periods (lying down, reading, or watching TV).

PARENTS >> When my daughter was this age, she would sometimes get invited to a sleepover party the night before a game, but we all know how little sleeping happens at those! What I preferred was for my daughter to have a friend on the same team come over to our house if she wanted to do a sleepover before a big game.

That way, we knew they would go to bed at a reasonable time and wake up early and ready to play. That is a form of recovery.

Another thing to keep in mind is that the first 30-45 minutes following the first game in a 2-game set is the most important for the body's recovery. Make sure you've already planned what to feed them so you can get food and fluids into their system, and then they can play a bit with their friends before the next game starts. But do not let them go chasing after their teammates or running around in the first half hour or so; you need to make sure their body gets proper nutrition at the right time so they are ready for the next game. *–Walid*

MENTALITY

Being a better athlete does not necessarily mean training harder or longer. Certainly a youth soccer player must spend time physically preparing her body to meet the demands of a practice session or game. Similarly, engaging in **MENTAL PREPARATION** can help her perform at a higher level by creating the proper mindset for either practice or a game.

At Level 1, a youth soccer player should be playing for the love of the game. While she may possess a competitive spirit and WANT to win, she should always remember that she is there to have fun.

NOTE >> If soccer is not fun for a youth soccer player, she will probably not achieve higher levels of performance. Likewise, if she's playing soccer simply because her parents want her to participate in a sport and not because she actually enjoys the game, she may not continue playing at higher levels of competition.

HOW TO MENTALLY PREPARE TO PLAY OR PRACTICE SOCCER »

- Take a few minutes to think about the game or practice you're about to engage in.
- Close your eyes and take a few deep breaths. As you slowly breathe in and out, picture yourself breathing in the fresh air as you run around the field.
- Think about the friends you have on the team and try to remember something funny or nice they recently said to you.
- Think about how much you like your teammates and respect your coaches, and vow to play your best for them—and for yourself.

COACHES » Starting at the younger ages and going on up through high school, I start relating soccer practice to school, because the girls can relate to school more than anything since that's the one thing they do five days a week. When they first come to practice, they've had a full day and want to share their stories with each other, so there is a lot of chatter going on. I tell them they can take the first few minutes while stretching to talk and get it all out of their systems. But once I say practice has started, all the chatter I hear had better be related to soccer. I explain to them it is like being in class: When the bell rings, the focus needs to be on the teacher, the subject, and the assignments; it's no different here. It is very important to set this pattern of expectation for players at a young age because how well they pay attention and follow directions now sets the foundation of how they are going to do as athletes. –*Walid*

1.3 FITNESS

FITNESS matters A soccer player needs to develop strength and speed to play the game effectively and to prevent injuries. She also needs a high degree of mobility. Mobility is the ability to move through a full range of motion. A **COMPLETE ATHLETE** maintains a high degree of:

LOWER-BODY STRENGTH

UPPER-BODY STRENGTH

FLEXIBILITY / MOBILITY

CORE STRENGTH

SPEED / QUICKNESS / ENDURANCE

LOWER-BODY STRENGTH

LOWER-BODY STRENGTH is necessary for nearly any athletic activity. In soccer, a great deal of power and torque for kicking, stopping, and starting comes from the hamstrings, quadriceps, and gluteal muscles. Soccer players tend to be one-side dominant in their legs due to relying on their right or left foot mainly.

Exercises like single-leg squats and broad jumps can help a youth soccer player develop the leg strength, posture, and balance that lead to better soccer technique. Single-leg wall squats and single-leg wall sits can also help determine if one leg is stronger than the other and can be used to develop a better balance of strength in both legs. The broad jump is a great linear measurement of power in the legs.

TO PERFORM SINGLE-LEG SQUATS »

- Stand on one leg while your other leg is lifted off the ground in front of your body. Your hip should be bent to approximately 45 degrees and your knee bent to approximately 90 degrees.
- Hold your arms out straight in front of you with your hands clasped together. From this position, squat down until your knee is bent to approximately 60 degrees.
- Return to the start position and repeat.

TO PERFORM A SINGLE-LEG WALL SIT »

- Stand with your back against a smooth vertical wall and your feet approximately shoulder-width apart.
- Slowly slide your back down the wall until both knees and hips are at a 90-degree angle.

- Lift one foot off the ground and hold it as long as possible. After a period of rest, lift your other foot and hold it.

NOTE >> If you can hold one foot up considerably longer than the other, you may need to work on developing a better balance of strength in both legs.

TO PERFORM A BROAD JUMP >>

- Stand behind a line marked on the ground, with your feet slightly apart.
- Use a two-foot takeoff and landing, swinging your arms and bending your knees to provide forward drive.
- Jump as far as possible, landing on both feet without falling backwards.

UPPER-BODY STRENGTH

UPPER-BODY STRENGTH is also important for soccer, although it is not always the first thing people think of at this age. There is a popular belief that lifting weights can be bad for your health, stunt growth, or even cause you to get bulky. Studies have repeatedly shown the complete opposite of this, and proper strength training actually can help keep you from getting sick as often and promote healthier habits. Throughout the levels, we will test your ability to lift your body weight in exercises like the common push-up and pull-up. We will also check your upper-body strength by including tests such as throwing a small medicine ball.

UPPER-BODY STRENGTH IS DEVELOPED IN TWO DISTINCT WAYS »

PULL EXERCISES, in which you are pulling something toward your body, help increase upper-back strength and mobility. The bent-arm hold pull-up is just one type of pull exercise we will test you on to determine your strength.

PUSH EXERCISES, in which you are pushing something away from your body, are great for increasing strength and mobility in the chest and arms. Some of the best upper-body exercises are body-weight exercises like bent-arm hold pull-ups and push-ups. Bear in mind that bigger is not necessarily better. In fact, bulky upper body muscles can actually decrease mobility.

TO PERFORM A BENT-ARM HOLD PULL-UP »

- Grasp an overhead bar using an underhand grip (palms facing toward body).
- Position your body with your arms flexed and your chin clearing the bar. Your chest should be held close to the bar, with your legs hanging straight.
- Hold this position for as long as possible.

TO PERFORM PUSH-UPS »

- Lie face down on the floor (or mat) with your hands under your shoulders or slightly wider than your chest, fingers straight, legs straight and parallel.
- Straighten your arms, pushing your upper body up and keeping your back and knees straight.

- Bend your arms to lower your upper body until your elbows are at a 90-degree angle and your upper arms are parallel to the floor.
- Perform as many repetitions as possible without resting.

FLEXIBILITY / MOBILITY

A good degree of **FLEXIBILITY AND MOBILITY** leads to better soccer technique and helps to prevent injuries.

The sit-and-reach test is used to assess and improve a youth athlete's level of lower-body flexibility and mobility.

TO PERFORM THE SIT-AND-REACH TEST >>

NOTE >> You'll need a box that is 12 inches high, such as a milk crate. Tape a yardstick or ruler to the top so that the first 9 inches hang over the edge and the 9-inch mark is exactly on the edge against which you will place your feet.

- Place the box against a wall.
- Sit on the floor in front of the box with your legs straight in front of you and the soles of your feet flat against the front side of the box. (The overhanging part of the ruler should be pointed at your chest or midsection).
- Keeping your legs straight and flat on the floor, stretch forward and reach along the ruler with one hand on top of the other, palms down.
- Stretch forward three times without bouncing; then reach as far as possible, holding the farthest point for at least three seconds.

The purpose of the 90/90 test is to determine if you have tight hamstrings and are at risk of possible leg injury. A failure in this test means you need to stretch more to gain more flexibility.

TO PERFORM A 90/90 TEST »

- Lie on your back, legs straight and flat on the ground.
- Bend the test knee to 90 degrees and then raise it so your thigh is vertical and your knee still bent. (The non-test leg should still be straight and resting on the floor.)
- Bend at the knee to straighten your test leg. If you can extend your leg to 0 degrees (the entire leg is straight at a 90-degree angle from your body), you have passed. If you cannot straighten your leg, record what angle you have left to achieve neutral position (straight knee). Anything greater than 10 degrees is failing. (Make sure the non-test leg never bends or comes off the ground while measuring.)

CORE STRENGTH

Core muscles provide power and stability for every movement in soccer, including kicking, jumping, running, cutting, and throwing. The core is what transfers power into anything you are kicking. **CORE STRENGTH** is much more than sit-ups and crunches; the core muscles are located in the abdominal area, lower back, and glutes. Planks and low-back knee marches are some of the most effective core workouts; we will do timed tests of these throughout the levels.

TO PERFORM A PLANK »

- Get down on the floor with your hands slightly wider than shoulder-width apart and your arms straight and supporting your weight.
- Make sure your body stays straight; your hips shouldn't be sticking way up in the air or sagging.
- Hold this position for as long as you can.

TO PERFORM AN OVERHEAD MEDICINE-BALL THROW »

- Stand with both feet on a line, facing forward.
- Hold a medicine ball with both hands and raise it above and behind your head.
- Draw the ball back and throw it as far as possible out in front of you at a 45-degree angle.
- It is okay to follow through past the line after throwing.

SPEED / QUICKNESS / ENDURANCE

THERE ARE TWO TYPES OF SOCCER SPEED »

- Straightaway speed on an open field
- Lateral (side-to-side) quickness

The 30-yard sprint helps an athlete improve straightaway **SPEED**. The 5-10-5 shuttle run, or pro agility drill, is a great way to improve lateral **QUICKNESS**, because it helps to hone an athlete's ability to accelerate, decelerate, stop, and reaccelerate without losing balance. The beep test is a good way to measure and improve **ENDURANCE**.

TO PERFORM A 30-YARD SPRINT »

- Place two cones 30 yards apart.
- Starting at one cone, run as fast as you can to the other cone.

TO PERFORM A 5-10-5 SHUTTLE RUN »

- Set up three marker cones five yards apart.
- Start at the middle marker cone in a three-point stance.
- Turn and run five yards to the right side and touch the marker cone with your right hand.
- Turn around and run 10 yards to the left and touch the marker cone with your left hand.
- Turn and finish by running back to the middle marker cone.

TO PERFORM A BEEP TEST »

NOTE » You'll first need to download a beep test audio recording or beep test app, which will play beeps at set intervals. As the test proceeds, the interval between each successive beep reduces, forcing the athlete to increase her speed.

- Draw two lines 20 yards apart.
- Stand behind one of the lines, facing the second line and begin running when instructed by the recording.
- Continue running between the two lines, turning when signaled by the recorded beeps. After about one minute, a sound indicates an increase in speed, and the beeps will be closer together.
- The test is stopped when the athlete can no longer keep in sync with the recording.

LEVEL-1 FITNESS TEST

LOWER-BODY STRENGTH »

- Single-leg squats on each leg for 30 seconds each
- Broad jump 62 inches or more

UPPER-BODY STRENGTH »

- Flexed-arm hang of 15 seconds
- 25 push-ups in 60 seconds

FLEXIBILITY/MOBILITY »

- Sit-and-reach test score of at least 32 centimeters
- 90/90 test is pass or fail

CORE STRENGTH/BALANCE »

- Plank for 2 ½ minutes
- Single-leg balance on each leg for 30 seconds
- Standing overhead 6-pound medicine-ball throw of at least 4 yards.

SPEED/QUICKNESS/ENDURANCE »

- 5-10-5 shuttle run in 6.0 seconds
- 30-yard sprint time of 5.3 seconds
- Beep test minimum score of 5/2-6/4 (number of levels/ number of shuttles completed)

1.4 TECHNIQUE

In just about any sport, the basic **TECHNIQUES** are the most important skills to master. These skills are the building blocks upon which more advanced skills are learned. As a youth athlete achieves higher levels of success in soccer, she will begin to specialize in a particular position on the team.

A **COMPLETE ATHLETE** not only masters the basic and advanced skills needed to play the game, she also understands the roles and responsibilities of every position on a team and how all the positions work together to perform and win games. The basic skills of soccer include:

FOUNDATIONAL BALL SKILLS / DRIBBLING

PASSING

PUSH PASS

INSTEP PASS

OUTSIDE-OF-THE-FOOT PASS

BALL CONTROL

SHOOTING

HEADING

FOUNDATIONAL BALL SKILLS / DRIBBLING

- Change of direction/pace
- Shielding
- Close control/head up
- Learning vision/control between tight-space dribbling and open-space dribbling

TECHNICAL TIPS »

- Maintain control of the ball while moving at speed
- Move at a speed that is comfortable for you
- Keep your head up

COMMON MISTAKES »

- Looking down at the ball instead of focusing on your team's options
- Running too fast with the ball and over-dribbling
- Not distinguishing between big open areas and tight-space dribbling
- Relying on one foot and not using both feet

TECHNICAL TIPS »

- Toe taps
- Side to side—sole of the foot
- Push/pull—instep to sole
- V turn—both inside/inside-outside
- Cryuff Turn
- L turn—behind the leg
- Scissors
- Step over

TECHNICAL TIPS »

- Maintain control of the ball
- Control your speed
- Change of speed after the cut
- Timing of the cut

COMMON MISTAKES »

- Losing control of the ball
- Going too fast
- Wrong timing of the cut
- Not using both feet

PASSING

- Passing with all surfaces of the foot
- Push pass
- Instep pass
- Outside-the-foot pass

PUSH PASS

TECHNICAL TIPS »

- The inside of the foot remains square to the target throughout the entire motion
- The body is square to the target
- The supporting foot is pointed to the target
- Strike the middle of the ball with the inside of the foot

COMMON MISTAKES >>

- Planting the supporting foot behind the ball plane
- Planting the supporting foot too far away from the ball
- Not using both feet
- Not being balanced with the opposite arm and leg

INSTEP PASS

- Approach the ball from a slight angle
- Place the non-kicking foot alongside the ball, passing in the direction of the passer
- Drive diagonally across the ball, kicking the ball with the instep of the foot; the knee and the body should be over the ball at the time of contact
- Follow through low with the kicking foot
- Balance with the opposite leg and arm when striking the ball

COMMON MISTAKES >>

- Approaching the ball from the wrong angle
- Positioning the supporting foot incorrectly
- Failing to follow through
- Not using both feet

OUTSIDE-OF-THE-FOOT PASS

TECHNICAL TIPS »

- Point the striking foot down and in
- Lock the striking foot ankle
- Keep the knee of the kicking foot over the ball
- Keep the supporting foot behind the ball plane to allow room for the kicking foot movement

COMMON MISTAKES »

- Loss of balance
- Stretching for the ball

BALL CONTROL

- All surfaces
- First touch—directional
- Off the bounce
- On the move
- Out of the air

TECHNICAL TIPS >>

- Keep your eyes on the ball so you can quickly decide which body part will control the ball—chest, thigh, foot, or head
- If receiving the ball with the foot, keep the toes pointed up and the ankle locked
- If receiving the ball with a different body part, get the body in line with the direction of the ball
- Always come to meet the ball

COMMON MISTAKES »

- Being stiff when the ball arrives
- Misjudging the flight of the ball
- Allowing the ball to bounce up instead of controlling the ball down
- Not looking over your shoulder

SHOOTING

- All surfaces
- Inside the foot
- Instep/Driving
- Outside of the foot
- Accuracy to aim

TECHNICAL TIPS »

- Lean forward with the shoulders and place the kicking knee over the ball
- The kicking foot remains pointed diagonally across the ball
- Throughout the kicking motion, the supporting foot is pointed at the target
- The opposite hip of the non-kicking foot is your aim for accuracy
- Drive through the ball
- To keep the ball low, follow through the strike on the upper half of the ball

COMPLETE ATHLETE

JOIN THE CONVERSATION!
Download the Complete Athlete app now!

COMMON MISTAKES »

- Incorrect positioning of the supporting foot causing a loss of power and accuracy
- Failing to drive through
- Not keeping the ankle locked when striking the ball
- Using only one foot

HEADING

INTRODUCTION TO TECHNIQUE (BEING AGE APPROPRIATE) »

- Standing
- Jumping
- Attacking Headers
- Defensive Headers

TECHNICAL TIPS »

- Assess the flight of the ball
- Time the jump to head the ball at the highest point
- Keep eyes open
- Lock the neck and arch the back to snap through the ball with the head
- Thrust from the waist
- Use a technical snap to create power

COMPLETE ATHLETE

JOIN THE CONVERSATION!
Download the Complete Athlete app now!

COMMON MISTAKES »

- Closing eyes prior to contact
- Mistiming the jump
- Mistiming the technical snap of the head
- Positioning the feet incorrectly, causing poor balance

1.5 LIFESTYLE

As youth soccer players achieve higher levels of success, they will find the demands on their time increasing. Creating a healthy balance between sports, academics, family obligations, and social activities requires strong time-management skills and a clear understanding of what's important.

A **COMPLETE ATHLETE** prioritizes the various elements of her life as follows:

FAMILY

ACADEMICS

SOCIAL LIFE

ROLE MODEL

LIVING YOUR SPORT

FAMILY

Parents play a number of important roles in the lives of youth soccer players: At Level 1, parents serve as:

- Chauffeur, by driving to and from practices and games
- Financer, by paying for equipment, uniforms, team snacks, and more
- Cheerleader and spectator, by taking time out of their busy schedules to attend games and cheer their children on

Youth soccer players sometimes feel that being a soccer player is the most important part of their lives. They believe that everyone should drop everything to accommodate their sports activities. What they need to remember is that soccer may not be the most important part of their parents' lives. After all, parents have other responsibilities to take care of, such as jobs, other children, possibly their own parents, and themselves.

Youth soccer players must remember to show appreciation for all the things their parents do to support them as they move up the levels of play. They do this by not acting as if they're the center of attention and by finding ways to help their parents out.

DO YOU ACT LIKE YOU'RE THE CENTER OF ATTENTION?

Do your parents get stressed out when you "suddenly" remember you have to be somewhere? Have any of your siblings missed an activity because you "had" to attend a special practice session that your coach told you about the week before, but that you forgot to mention until five minutes before you had to leave for it?

If these are common occurrences for you, you need to make some changes. You need to open your eyes and start paying attention to the needs of others. For example, keep your parents apprised of any changes to your practice schedule. Let's say your sister has a music lesson every Tuesday afternoon. If your coach schedules a special practice on a Tuesday afternoon, arrange to get a ride with a teammate so that your mom can get your sister to her lesson on time.

LOOK FOR WAYS TO HELP YOUR PARENTS WHEN POSSIBLE »

Your parents devote an enormous amount of their time taking you to and from games and practices, buying you equipment, watching you play, and cheering you on. When they get home, they have many responsibilities waiting for them, including cooking meals, cleaning the house, doing laundry, helping with homework, and more.

When you take on a few chores, such as keeping your room clean or doing the dishes after dinner, you're lessening some of the burden on your parents' shoulders and at the same time showing gratitude for all they do for you.

PARENTS » As a parent of a Level-1 player, I expect that on Friday and Saturday nights, she will have her backpack set by her bed with her uniforms, socks, shin guards, cleats, and everything she needs for the next day's games ready to go. It is her responsibility to have her bag ready when I say "Let's go!" in the morning. When we get home from her games on Saturday, the first thing she does is go into the laundry room to wash her uniforms and then she puts them back in her backpack for Sunday's games.

As a parent, you've got to teach your child it's her responsibility to be game-ready. She needs to be focused enough on her game that she is already thinking about what uniforms and equipment she needs to be ready, and she needs to share with you any changes to the schedule for the next day. Children this age are old enough to stay on top of their readiness and to relay information to you. Parents just need to make sure they have laid the right foundation and stressed the importance of taking responsibility, and that they are trusting their children to rise to the task. *–Walid*

CAMILLE LEVIN >> *My parents were my biggest supporters; they saw me at my happiest and at my saddest. Even though they didn't understand all the rules and intricacies of soccer (at least, not at first), they knew me and they knew when I was giving 100% and when I wasn't. If I had a really good game, they were the first to compliment me for it. If it was a hard day and I was really emotional or upset after a game, they were pretty quiet. They wouldn't start attacking me or say I could have done better. They just let me know they were proud of me no matter what and gave me the space to feel however I needed to.*

A lot of times in youth games, you see the parents going crazy on the sidelines, yelling at their kids, and that really impacts the kids themselves because it makes them self-conscious and distracted about what their parents might say or do. Sometimes you even see parents yelling at other people's children. I strongly believe that the only thing that should come from parents on the sidelines is encouragement; it's not their place to be coaches. My parents would offer me critiques in the car after the game, if I needed it, but it was in a private space and it was never an attack or a way of putting me down. It was just them expressing their honest opinion on what they saw. I disagreed with them sometimes, but I always knew they were looking out for my best interest and were never overly aggressive in any way on the field or off.

ACADEMICS

Many youth soccer players (and many parents as well) have the misconception that if an athlete is good enough, grades don't matter. Nothing could be further from the truth. For one thing, college coaches know that athletes who perform well in school—as well as on the field of play—are generally mature individuals with good time-management skills. These are the student-athletes the coaches want in their programs.

As a youth soccer player travels the path toward becoming a **COMPLETE ATHLETE**, she must develop a lifestyle that allows her to maintain good grades. Granted, not everyone is going to be an A+ student, but a few key strategies can go a long way toward helping improve grades.

STRATEGIES FOR MAINTAINING GOOD GRADES >>

HAND IN ALL ASSIGNMENTS ON TIME. Most teachers make a deduction for homework turned in late.

BE ORGANIZED. Having all your materials organized

can help you complete your assignments on time.

PAY CLOSE ATTENTION IN CLASS. Focus on what the teacher is saying, take good notes and follow directions.

STUDY A LITTLE BIT EVERY DAY. Just as practicing drills can help improve your soccer skills, regular studying time helps you retain information better.

ASK QUESTIONS. Your teachers want you to succeed; if you're having trouble with the material, your teacher is the first person you should go to for help.

DON'T CRAM FOR TESTS. Put in extra study time at least a few days before the exam. Read through textbook chapters, study your notes, and take any practice tests available to you.

BEHAVE APPROPRIATELY IN CLASS. Good behavior starts with knowing the rules. In school, the rules usually include sitting still at your desk, listening to your teacher, and raising your hand if you want to speak. Other schools may have other rules, but generally speaking, knowing— and obeying—these rules automatically leads to good behavior.

COACHES » One year, just a week before the league championship game, I had a parent ask me if we could speak after practice. I agreed, and at the end of the day, we stepped aside and she explained to me that, as much as it hurt her, her daughter would not be playing that weekend in our big game. It turns out that her daughter had had a very rough semester and flunked her final exam, so her parents were taking away all of her privileges and everything she enjoyed—including soccer, which was her life—until she got her grades back up.

That parent may have been worried that I would protest but, in fact, she had my complete support. Clearly, those parents knew the magnitude of teaching a child at a young age how to balance academics and sports. After all, for anyone serious about having an athletic career, the ultimate goal is to have sports and academics go hand in hand, because that's how you'll get into and stay in college.

The next day, when I explained to the rest of the team why that young lady was not with us, it really shook some of her teammates that I supported the decision 100% and was on the same page as the parents. Two weeks later, after the girl buckled down and ended up passing her classes, I had a really great talk with her about how important it was for her to stay on top of her academics and keep her grades up. Her parents had taught her a painful but memorable lesson by taking the game away from her—and I don't think she ever forgot it. –Ziad

COACHES » These days, by the time an athlete reaches middle school, the homework load has become much heavier. A player needs to learn how to balance her practice schedule with her academics. It is extremely important that coaches point out to their players that, without the grades, sports will not be an option in the future. In high school and college, students are not eligible to play if they don't maintain a certain grade-point average.

When my own daughter was that age, her practice days were Tuesday and Thursday, so her homework schedule was different on those days. She got home at 3:30, had a snack and then she did homework from 4 to 5:30, when it was time to head to practice. This routine was non-negotiable; she just knew that she didn't have time to waste after school on Tuesdays and Thursdays. Some players on other teams lived up to 45 minutes away, and many of them worked on homework or studying while in the car. The most important thing is that coaches understand and respect the priority of academics, and stress to their players the need for a good schedule on practice days. Athletics should never be an excuse for why homework was not completed. *–Walid*

SOCIAL LIFE

A solid **SOCIAL LIFE** is important for all young people, not just youth athletes. Friends provide companionship and recreation. Friends also give advice to one another and often help to ease anxiety during times of stress. Young people who don't have friends tend to be more lonely and unhappy. They also have lower levels of academic achievement and lower self-esteem.

While many youth soccer players' social lives revolve around their teammates, many have friends outside of sports. Either way, a soccer player's lifestyle should include spending time with friends outside of soccer and learning to be considerate of those friends.

HOW TO MAKE FRIENDS OUTSIDE OF SOCCER »

There are many ways to make friends outside of soccer. You are surrounded by potential friends in school, in your neighborhood, and even at your church or temple. By opening your eyes and really observing other kids, you can find mutual likes (or even dislikes) to bond over.

For example, you may notice another kid wearing a jersey representing your favorite team. By saying to that person, "Hey, I like that team, too," you make a connection to a potential friend. Asking questions to get to know the other person can help create a true friendship.

HOW TO BE CONSIDERATE OF FRIENDS' TIME AND OTHER OBLIGATIONS >>

Whether you develop friendships with your teammates or your classmates, you need to remember that everyone has responsibilities. They have homework to do, sports or music to practice, siblings to babysit, and chores to complete.

Sometimes you'll make plans with a friend, only to have him or her cancel at the last minute. It may be because they forgot about a family event, or their parents scheduled something and forgot to tell them about it. It may even be because they suddenly realized they needed more time to get a school assignment finished.

Whatever the reason, being considerate of your friends means not getting angry or throwing a fit when plans change or when they just can't seem to find the time to be with you. Be understanding and remember that next time it might be you having to cancel at the last minute.

PARENTS >> Watching my daughter grow up, one of the things I really have come to admire about her is how she has balanced her life and the kinds of friends she has: friends from soccer, from church, and from school.

She has never said, "That's it. These are my soccer friends and that's who I am going to hang around with 24/7." Going to school, she made friends there and spends time with them. Going to church, she made friends there and spends time with them. Going to soccer, she made great friends there, and she makes time for them, too. The bottom line of it all is that balancing life and creating friends in every circle teaches young people how to manage different circles. Their friends from each area of their lives are going to have different approaches, different problems, different opinions and ideas, and different stuff to do for fun.
–Walid

ROLE MODEL

A **ROLE MODEL** is someone who possesses qualities that others admire. They are the people others look up to and want to be like. Being a good role model is another attribute that college and professional coaches like to see in the athletes they recruit.

Role models demonstrate respect for others and for themselves. To be a good role model, start by demonstrating respect for others by:

- Listening carefully, not interrupting and fidgeting when someone else is speaking
- Addressing people by their names
- Valuing other people's opinions
- Letting teammates know they are appreciated
- Not insulting people, making fun of them, or talking about them behind their backs

PARENTS AND COACHES >> One of the most important things we need to do as coaches and as parents is to paint the picture for these players of how to become great role models. I love inviting players and parents to watch older teams play and look for certain behaviors in those players and teams. How do the players talk to one another? How do they interact on the field? What do their attitudes seem like? How closely is everyone paying attention to the coach at half-time? Seeing those traits demonstrated really allows younger players to get a clear sense of how to behave the same way, and it also reinforces for the parents the right way that their child should be conducting herself. *–Ziad*

LIVING YOUR SPORT

Youth soccer players who are serious about getting a college scholarship and possibly playing soccer professionally are generally committed to practicing more and doing whatever they can to improve their skills and physical fitness. Many also cultivate a lifestyle in which they "live their sport."

Some youth soccer players may never be seen without a ball in their hands. Others may spend time watching professional soccer matches live or on television. Still others may spend time reading about their favorite players to learn what they've done to succeed.

HOW TO LIVE YOUR SPORT >>

At Level 1, a youth soccer player begins to live her sport simply by playing for the love of the game. She should make it a priority to have fun and to bond with other girls who share her love of the game.

MIA HAMM

As early as possible, parents should try to find the proper, age-appropriate balance between how much they should be involved and how much they should step back and let the child learn how to handle things. Sometimes you see parents who want involvement in the sport far more than the child does, or vice-versa; other times, you see children who want to participate but have no interest in taking any personal responsibility and just rely on the parents to do absolutely everything. I believe that it needs to be a collaborative effort: Children need to learn how to take initiative for themselves gradually, and parents need to learn when to carry, when to push, and when to step back. It's a process, but it's a vital part of raising a complete athlete.

Another important thing to remember is the child, parent, and coaches each have a different perspective and experience with each practice or game. Most children go from being a competitor back to being a kid as soon as they get in the car to go home; they tend to leave the game on the field and move on to the next thing easily. They might be sad about a loss or a practice that didn't go well, but they generally don't dwell on those disappointments. As a child just learning the game and figuring out how all the different rules and techniques work together, you are usually just doing the best you can to keep up with the ball and trying to score or strip the ball from your opponent. And when the game is over, you're not worried about its implications.

Parents, on the other hand, don't seem to be able to make the switch from "parent-spectator" to just "parent" nearly as quickly. My parents liked to discuss the games on the way home—why one player made the decisions she did or what a team's style of play was like. Sometimes, that made me really uncomfortable as I listened. I appreciated that they cared about my sport, but sometimes it felt as if that was the only thing on their minds. It was difficult to put into words at that age, but I often felt disloyal to a teammate or coach if we were dissecting his or her performance on the field, because when you're young, you base your decisions on what you see, not necessarily what you have experienced—because it probably hasn't been much by that point. In other words, you are making the best call you can in the moment, rather than thinking about big picture or strategy. Often, that leads to choices that a more mature player might not have made, and parents often forget that. I would encourage parents to show their enthusiasm and excitement for their children during the game, but not to allow the game to follow you home.

The same is true of coaches. Of course your job is to educate your players about the hows and whys of the game; but at this level, it is too much to ask them to stick around for a long time after a game to rehash all the plays or enter into a deep analysis of what won or lost the game for your team. That deeper post-game analysis is your job as a coach, but it is simply not where your team is.

Parents and coaches would be well-served to keep this in mind. Your involvement, excitement, and investment are admirable, and I applaud you for that! But in your effort to show interest, please don't lose sight of the fact that children sometimes have a better grasp than we do on the fact that it is just a game and that there are other things worth focusing on when it's all over.

IN LEVEL 2

a soccer player is starting to develop her own personality on and off the field. Foundational skills are being refined with dedicated practice and new skills are being learned. Off the field, you begin to understand how attitude, preparation, and lifestyle can play a role in preparing you for higher levels. Mastering this level isn't just for athletes, though; coaches and parents will learn how to support athletes and appreciate the importance of balancing their involvement in encouraging their daughters to reach their full potential.

2.1 ATTITUDE

A **POSITIVE ATTITUDE** is essential to an athlete's success both on and off the playing field, especially as she moves into higher levels of play. In fact, college coaches seek out athletes who display positive attitudes.

A positive attitude can be developed with practice, just like any other skill. A **COMPLETE ATHLETE** makes a habit of demonstrating the following five attributes:

RESPECT

SPORTSMANSHIP

TEAMWORK

PROFESSIONALISM

LEADERSHIP

RESPECT

RESPECT means treating others in ways that show they have worth and value, and being considerate of other people's feelings. At Level 1, all youth soccer players should treat their coaches with respect. That does not change at Level 2. In fact, a **COMPLETE ATHLETE** always shows respect for her coaches at every level of play.

At Level 2, it's important for youth soccer players to learn to respect their teammates as well. The key is to treat them the way you would like them to treat you.

HOW TO DEMONSTRATE RESPECT FOR YOUR TEAMMATES AND OPPONENTS »

- Learn your teammates' names and address them by their names.
- Listen carefully when a teammate is talking to you.
- Do not insult teammates or opponents or talk about them behind their backs.
- Forgive others when they make a mistake and do not make fun of them.
- Let your teammates know you appreciate them both on and off the field.

ATHLETES » In the ages between 11 and 14, it is so important to learn how to respect your teammates and to set the tone so that everyone on the team feels that they will be treated the same regardless of their level of play.

There was a game when a forward missed a shot and another player said to her, "I can't believe you missed that! How could you not have scored?" At half-time, I sat them both down and said, "I'm going to ask you a question: Do you think she wanted to miss that shot?" The first girl, of course, said no. So I continued, "Then why would you tell her that you can't believe she missed the shot?" The girl immediately apologized and said she hadn't meant it that way. That was great, but I continued: "What would have happened if you had told her she was a great player—do you think she would have been mentally in a better position to score?" She said yes, so I then asked her, "Would you have liked it if someone had told you they couldn't believe you missed a tackle? Just think about what happened, what you said, and the impact on your teammate and on the game."

Teach players about the impact of what they say and how they should interact with one another. They all fall on the same page, and they need to understand how important it is to have respect for their teammates. Being positive and just saying something as simple as, "Good job!" can affect the game and do so much more to improve your teammates' performance than any kind of negativity.
—Ziad

**COMPLETE
ATHLETE**

JOIN THE CONVERSATION!
Download the Complete Athlete app now!

SPORTSMANSHIP

GOOD SPORTSMANSHIP starts with respect for one's teammates, opponents, coaches, and officials. At Level 1, all youth soccer players should know the basic rules of soccer and always play by them. That does not change at Level 2. In fact, a **COMPLETE ATHLETE** always plays by the rules at every level of play.

At Level 2, youth soccer players begin to differentiate themselves by their skill levels. They begin to develop high expectations for themselves as well as for their teammates. Often, it's the players that put in the most effort in terms of **PREPARATION** that play the best. However, some girls who practice regularly and try hard may not develop beyond a certain skill level. At Level 2, youth soccer players learn to accept players who have different levels of ability.

HOW TO TREAT TEAMMATES WHO ARE LESS SKILLED THAN YOU »

- Never make fun of or insult a teammate.
- Do not talk about them behind their backs.
- Acknowledge any good plays they make.
- Reassure them if they make a poor play.
- Encourage them to improve by practicing skills with them outside of regular team practices.

ATHLETES » Something I like to do with my 12- and 13-year-old players is to challenge them: "Define for me what makes a player great." They always give me the same answers: someone who can score, who is talented, who is the best at what they do.

Nope. A great player is one who makes everyone else play and perform better than they would otherwise. That's the definition of a great player.

It is essential at these ages to teach that, because this is the age where gaps start to open on the team between one or two extremely great players and the rest. It is so important for the stars to realize that their gift is one that needs to be shared, and it is important for the rest of the team to realize that the leaders should be lifting up everyone else with them.

A few years ago, I was at a soccer camp where the kids came in for a week and played soccer, but they did a number of other activities as well. We would have practice for an hour in the morning and then pickup games at night, and on Wednesday night there was a girl on my team who happened to play on a national team. At that pickup game, her team won 10-0, and she scored all the goals—just one after another. I didn't comment on it; I just told her I needed to talk to her after the game. I explained that God gave her a talent to share with other people instead of just keeping it for her own fame and that the next day, her goal needed to be to share the ball and help the other kids enjoy the game by passing to them and involving them, too.

The following evening, she was on my team again, and I didn't say a word about the day before; I just sent the girls out to start the game. Through that whole game, she passed the ball to everyone else and let everyone else do the scoring. She was dribbling and then setting up the other kids for success and passing the ball to them. Afterward, she stayed and helped me clean up the field. I asked her if she felt better after that game than the one the day before. She nodded and said, "Thank you, Coach. I get it."

I told her I was proud of her and added, "Just don't forget this. That smile that you put on the faces of these kids will stay with them for a long, long time. They will always remember you for what you did for them in that game."

–Ziad

COACHES » You have to teach your team how to be good sports. One of the first things I teach my teams is that if anyone gets injured—our side or an opponent—to kick the ball out so the game is stopped and the player can be attended to.

One of the best things I have ever seen one of our teams do was at the age-13 State Cup, an opponent took a bad fall and ended up tearing her ACL. The first thing my players did when they saw she was in pain was kick the ball out, and then after after she got help, our girls sat down, held hands, and prayed for her. Even the opposing team's parents and coaches commented on that. It was a tremendous display of sportsmanship and the sort of thing that builds your reputation both on and off the field. It was one of my proudest moments as a coach.

–Ziad

JOIN THE CONVERSATION!
Download the Complete Athlete app now!

COMPLETE
ATHLETE

TEAMWORK

TEAMWORK means working together as a group in order to achieve a goal. In sports, players contribute their individual skills and efforts in cooperation with their teammates to win games. Learning to play as part of a team, and not just as an individual athlete, is important at every level of play.

At Level 2, soccer coaches may add team-building exercises to practice sessions. Youth soccer players need to take these exercises seriously. Learning how to trust each other helps teammates work together more effectively and, ultimately, to win more games.

COACHES » Something I love doing at this age is to make sure that everyone gets a chance to develop their skills. Too often, coaches rely on the one or two star players and the team follows suit, so that everyone is depending on those players and only those players really grow.

What I like to do is to create a couple of challenges that don't knock down my stars but that help them to understand the importance of being team players. At practice, I will tell a star, "You're very fast at dribbling, but I'm going to give you a 20-yard head start in a 50-yard sprint, and I guarantee I will beat you."

All the girls start laughing as we line up, but I wait until the star gets to the 40-yard line, and then I just kick the ball. It goes sailing across the line ahead of her, and everyone looks at me like I'm crazy. "Did you see that?" I say. "Nobody is faster than the ball."

I have the star player come back, and then I tell her, "This time, I want you to dribble with the ball for 50 yards. I'm going to give you a 10-yard head start, and this time I'm going to run and beat you." So we start over, put the balls on the ground at our feet, and she dribbles out to the 10- or 15-yard line, and then I just sprint without the ball and, of course, I get there first. "Do you get what I'm trying to tell you?" I ask. "It's much faster to run without the ball than with the ball. My point is that if you learn how to share the ball and pick up moments when to dribble or not, that's when you become a more effective player. You've got to learn how to use your teammates. It's much easier to find one of your teammates while you're dribbling, pass the ball to them, sprint without the ball, get the ball back, and then dribble than it is to dribble the whole 40 yards by yourself."

I've found that this is a very valuable exercise in helping to make everyone realize the importance of passing and working together, rather than just always deferring to the best player. It does this in a way that does not make the star player feel belittled or like she is being punished for being good. *–Walid*

JOIN THE CONVERSATION!
Download the Complete Athlete app now!

PROFESSIONALISM

Certainly a youth athlete is not a professional in the sense of being paid to play. However, developing the attitude and behaviors of a **PROFESSIONAL** can help her more easily move up through the levels.

At Level 1, a youth soccer player learns to arrive on time with all her equipment at hand. However, it's likely that her parents have helped her to do so by regularly washing her uniform and helping her keep track of her equipment.

At Level 2, a youth soccer player should begin to take responsibility for keeping her equipment clean and well maintained and for washing and folding her uniform properly. At this age, she should also take responsibility for her personal hygiene by showering regularly and always wearing deodorant so she can arrive at practices and games well groomed and ready to go to work.

COACHES >> At this level, coaches need to stress to the players that it is each girl's responsibility to have her gear with her at all times—it's no one else's responsibility but her own.

At one of my games, we had to change to our alternate jerseys because our primary jerseys were very similar in color to those of the opposing team. One girl opened her bag and didn't have her extra jersey with her, and her first response was, "My mom didn't put it in my bag."

We had an extra jersey, but I specifically sat her out the whole first half because I had told the team, "It is your responsibility at this age to check your bag and make sure you have your primary jersey, your alternate jersey, your two socks, and all your gear in your bags. It is not your mom's or dad's responsibility anymore." I explain it to them like this: "Can you show up to class and say, 'I'm sorry, teacher. I don't have my math book today because my mom didn't put it in my backpack'? Of course not." At this age, players should be checking on their own gear, their own water or Gatorade, their own cleats—they should not be waiting on their parents to get it for them or have it ready. *–Ziad*

KASSI MCCLUSKIE » *It is important to find a coach for whom you really enjoy playing and with whom you mesh well … but there is also a great benefit in learning how to play for all different kinds of coaches. I've had coaches who were unbelievably nice and easy-going, and I've had coaches who were unbelievably intense and cutthroat when it came to competition—and I am glad that I experienced both kinds. The different approaches not only brought out different strengths and helped me develop in different areas, but all those different coaching styles I experienced really helped me to shape my own leadership philosophy.*

Everyone responds differently to different kinds of motivation and discipline. You should never stand for a coach who is abusive, but don't automatically write off one who is different than a previous coach or your preferred style. Give him or her a chance and be willing to be coachable. You might be surprised by the new ways you grow!

LEADERSHIP

A good **LEADER** is able to inspire and motivate others to do things they would not normally do, or to perform better than they would on their own. Developing leadership skills can benefit a youth athlete not only in high school and college, but also in her professional life.

At Level 1, a youth soccer player begins to develop an understanding of what it takes to be an effective leader by watching how her coaches inspire and motivate her and her teammates. At Level 2, she can begin to display some of the leadership skills she has observed by looking out for and encouraging the less talented players on the team. For instance, she may invite a less talented player to work with her outside of a regular practice session.

CAMILLE LEVIN >> *Confidence can be a real struggle for preteen and teenage girls, but for me, confidence came from being on the soccer field. That has always been my happy place—whatever else is going on, that was my happy place. I think it's part of why I thrived on the field, because I was always enjoying myself. If I had ever stopped feeling that way, I would have stopped playing. It has always been about the happiness for me, not the money (because there really isn't much!) or the fame or some crazy lifestyle. Sure, I've gotten to see and experience some incredible things and I've met some amazing people all because of soccer, but at the end of the day, I am playing because I love the sport. I think if I had ever found myself consistently dreading it rather than loving it, I would have walked away. And someday, when joy is no longer the dominant emotion I feel when playing soccer, I will know that it is time to move on.*

2.2 PREPARATION

You will recall from Level 1 that **PREPARATION** refers to off-the-field activities, such as practicing skills, eating right, staying hydrated, getting enough rest, and mentally preparing for a game or practice. Coaches love athletes who prepare. These are the players who are eager to learn, eager to play and, ultimately, eager to win. They are the athletes that coaches want to help succeed, because they already have a winning attitude. Preparation also helps athletes feel positive and confident in their ability to perform.

A **COMPLETE ATHLETE** prepares to perform on the field of play by continuously improving on the following:

PRACTICE

NUTRITION

HYDRATION

RECOVERY

MENTALITY

PRACTICE

At Level 1, a youth soccer player practices the basic techniques of soccer with an emphasis on having fun and becoming a better, more confident player. At Level 2, a youth soccer player continues to work on mastering the basic techniques through individual practice sessions. She also begins to work on becoming a well-rounded player by understanding—and practicing—all positions involved in the game of soccer. Learning all the different positions also helps the youth soccer player begin to narrow down her choices for which positions to specialize in at higher levels of play.

As in Level 1, the more focused a youth athlete remains during her individual practice sessions, the more effective the practice time will be. **The idea is to work smarter—not harder or longer.** Creating a practice schedule with specific drills can help a youth soccer player focus better during the practice session.

LEVEL 2 SAMPLE PRACTICE SESSION >>

- Warm up and stretch
- Drill 1 — based on position skills
- Drill 2 — based on position skills
- Drill 3 — based on position skills

PRIVATE COACHING Starting at Level 2, a youth soccer player who is serious about moving into higher levels of play and possibly earning a scholarship for college should consider working with a private coach. Working with a private coach for the basic techniques can give a youth soccer player a huge advantage over other soccer players her age.

Most private coaches provide one-on-one sessions that are focused on the individual player and the skills she needs to improve most. They generally work on ball mastery, balance, agility, speed, tactical understanding, and decision-making to help a soccer player reach her maximum potential.

ATHLETES >> At this level, we see players starting to develop a real love of the game and a commitment to spending more time practicing. Often times they will show up early to practice to try to get more time in shooting before everyone else arrives. Often they will call up some friends and get together to practice crosses and passing, or play "soccer tennis" in groups of two or four.

Athletes will often want to start with some private coaching, almost like a tutor for schoolwork, in order to really hone their skills. This is great, but also remember that there is no better coach than the wall—it is one of the best ways for athletes to squeeze in a little practice time almost any time. Ten minutes spent practicing kicking against the wall can be incredibly helpful in working on reflexes, footwork, and speed.

Practice has to be taken more seriously at this stage; come prepared to practice, be focused in practice, and really learn from other players who are better. One of the best things that you can do as an athlete is to pair up with a more advanced player so that every drill is a challenge and requires "playing up" to a higher level.

NUTRITION

NUTRITION plays a key role in athletic performance. Youth athletes are building muscle, burning calories, and growing. They need to eat and drink regularly to make up for the loss of calories they are burning and the fluids they are using during practice and actual games.

An active youth soccer player needs to consume healthy food and beverages in order to:

- Replenish her energy supply
- Maintain hydration
- Obtain the vitamins and minerals needed to support metabolism, tissue growth, and repair
- Prevent injuries and/or illnesses
- Perform at her best both on and off the field

GENERAL SPORTS NUTRITION GUIDELINES »

- All athletes should consume 5 or more balanced meals spread throughout the day, every 3-4 hours.
- Meals should be eaten 2-3 hours before practice or games, and snacks eaten 1-1 $^1/_2$ hours before practice or games.
- Eat when you're hungry to prevent lean-muscle breakdown; stop when you're full to prevent being sluggish.
- Eat breakfast within 30 minutes of waking up to prevent lean-muscle breakdown, increase energy and concentration, and maintain good blood-sugar control. Choose whole grains, fresh fruit, and lean protein for breakfast.

- Eat well-balanced meals and snacks, consisting of carbohydrates, lean proteins, and heart-healthy fats.
- Drink a protein shake, or eat a snack or meal that has equal amounts of protein and carbohydrates, within 30 minutes after a workout.
- Choose fresh, whole foods when possible (instead of processed foods that are packaged or refined) to increase nutritional value. Avoid foods that are high in sugar and/or trans fat.

LEVEL-2 ATHLETE NUTRITION GUIDELINES »

Each individual has different macronutrient needs, based on height, weight, age, activity level, and genetic background. The following macronutrient guidelines are based on age and estimated activity level for a Level-2 athlete:

- 55% carbohydrate
- 20% protein
- 25% fat
- No more than 7% saturated fat
- No trans fat
- 31 grams of fiber per day
- No more than 150 calories per day from sugar (37.5 grams or 9 teaspoons)

Just as in Level 1, a Level-2 youth soccer player should choose from the following to fulfill the macronutrient needs listed above:

CARBOHYDRATES High fiber foods, such as whole-grain bread, brown rice, whole grain pasta (or gluten-free versions), beans, starchy vegetables (e.g., corn, peas, potatoes), quinoa, and cereal

PROTEINS Chicken, turkey, or fish, especially wild salmon, tuna, trout, mackerel, and sardines, which are high in heart-healthy omega-3 fatty acids

FATS Low-fat cheese, nuts/nut butters (natural peanut butter or almond butter), avocado, seeds, and heart-healthy oils like extra-virgin olive oil, canola oil, grapeseed oil, and flaxseed oil

VEGETABLES Preferably leafy green vegetables

ATHLETES » At this level, games are longer than at younger ages, and the field is bigger, too. That means your body is going to require a lot more fuel to burn. Nutrition is more important than ever now, so you need to focus on what you eat and how much you drink in the days leading up to game, just before the game, during the game, and after the game. If you want to keep up at this higher level, you have to give your body what it needs.

COMPLETE
ATHLETE

JOIN THE CONVERSATION!
Download the Complete Athlete app now!

HYDRATION

All athletes need to drink water before, during, and after practices and games. This is especially important on days when both temperatures and humidity levels are high. If a youth soccer player does not drink enough water, she could suffer from dehydration.

HOW TO MAINTAIN PROPER HYDRATION*>>

- Before exercise, drink 16-20 full ounces within the 2-hour period prior to exercise
- During exercise, drink 4-6 full ounces
- After exercise, replace 24 full ounces for every one pound of body weight lost during exercise
- * *Adapted from guidelines provided by the American College of Sports Medicine (ACSM)*

ATHLETES AND PARENTS >> Players should take responsibility for following the guidelines on how much to drink before, during, and after games; parents should be monitoring to make sure it's done the right way. If a player did not hydrate right ahead of time, she is not going to perform her best; if she did, and if she keeps up with her water intake during the game, she should be able to last through the whole game and perform very well.

COMPLETE
ATHLETE

JOIN THE CONVERSATION!
Download the Complete Athlete app now!

RECOVERY

Youth soccer players need to eat and drink within 30 minutes of a practice or game to make up for the calories they are burning and fluids they are using. Replenishing calories and fluids also aids in muscle recovery and repair.

HOW TO REPLENISH CALORIES AND FLUIDS »

- Drink 24 ounces of fluid for every pound of sweat lost within a 2-hour period of a game or practice
- Consume 15 grams of protein plus an equal amount of carbohydrates within the 30-minute recovery window

SLEEP Just as increased activity creates a greater need for calories, it also creates a greater need for sleep. An athlete's body does its growing, healing, and muscle repairing during sleep. **RECOVERY** also means allowing the body to rest and heal from the demands of practices and games.

According to the National Sleep Foundation, a Level-2 youth athlete should get 10–11 hours of sleep each night for proper growth and development. If that's not possible, or if she needs additional recovery time, she should look at her weekly schedule and plan how she can incorporate additional sleep or rest time. To get the additional rest she needs, she can take short naps (no longer than 30 minutes) or engage in quiet rest periods (lying down, reading, or watching TV).

ATHLETES » One weekend, my daughter's team had a tournament, and after the Saturday night game, she had a few friends over to stay the night. They decided to watch a movie and the next thing I knew, they were munching away on a bunch of junk and just loading up on unhealthy stuff. They went to bed and got up early, but the next morning when we got to the field for warm-ups, they were absolutely dragging. They could barely run, barely move. I could see such a difference between them and the players who had taken care of their nutrition properly the night before; it was so obvious. Recovery is so important. Pay attention to when you drink, how much you have, what you eat, and how long you sleep in order to be ready. –Walid

MENTALITY

Being a better athlete does not necessarily mean training harder or longer. Certainly a youth soccer player must spend time physically preparing her body to meet the demands of a practice session or game. Similarly, engaging in **MENTAL PREPARATION** can help her perform at a higher level by creating the proper mindset for either practice or a game.

At Level 1, a youth soccer player mentally prepares by closing her eyes, breathing deeply, and envisioning herself having fun on the soccer field. This is also a great activity to practice at Level 2. In addition, a youth soccer player should engage in activities that help her build confidence in her own abilities and that push her to higher levels of performance.

HOW TO BUILD CONFIDENCE ››

- Reflect on all the positive feedback you've gotten from your coaches.
- Tell yourself that you're a great player and a solid member of the team.
- Think about the constructive feedback you've gotten and remind yourself that those people really want to see you succeed.
- Disregard any negative comments (even if they're from your parents) and focus only on the positive comments.
- Don't beat yourself up when you make a mistake; instead, focus on doing better the next time.
- Continue to practice on your own. When you complete a successful practice session, your confidence rises. The more you practice, the higher your confidence will be.

COACHES » If I see that my team is all over the place in practice and the focus is not there, something I have found that works really well is to stop and have everyone lie down. I tell them, "Just lie on your back, and for the next two minutes, I want you to start visualizing what we are doing and what you can do to make it better." You can see an instant change in practice once they get up. It is a way to pull their mentality back to where it needs to be. As a coach, if you see that the mentality is not there, you need to harness the team back so that they can function as a unit. *–Walid*

ATHLETES » Every player is different in terms of how she mentally prepares for games. I had one player who, before every game, needed four minutes to lie down and simply focus on the game. Another player liked to take a couple of laps around the field on her own in order to gather her thoughts. *–Walid*

JOIN THE CONVERSATION!
Download the Complete Athlete app now!

⟨2.3⟩ FITNESS

FITNESS matters. A soccer player needs to develop strength and speed to play the game effectively and to prevent injuries. She also needs a high degree of mobility. Mobility is the ability to move through a full range of motion. A **COMPLETE ATHLETE** maintains a high degree of:

LOWER-BODY STRENGTH

UPPER-BODY STRENGTH

FLEXIBILITY / MOBILITY

CORE STRENGTH

SPEED / QUICKNESS / ENDURANCE

In Level 1, we discussed a number of exercises to improve a youth soccer player's overall fitness. At Level 2, a youth soccer player should be able to perform all Level-1 tests at a higher level in terms of time and distance. These exercises are revisited below, and several more exercises are introduced.

LOWER-BODY STRENGTH

LOWER-BODY STRENGTH is becoming more important than it might have been in Level 1. By putting more work into your lower-body strength you can begin to see significant speed gains and much quicker cutting and footwork. If lower-body strength is neglected, a soccer athlete can become predictably right- or left-leg dominant, which can be exposed by opponents.

Exercises like single-leg wall squats and broad jumps can help a youth soccer player develop the leg strength, posture, and balance that lead to better soccer technique. Single-leg wall squats and single-leg wall sits can also help determine if one leg is stronger than the other, and can be used to develop a better balance of strength in both legs.

TO PERFORM SINGLE-LEG SQUATS »

- Stand on one leg while your other leg is lifted off the ground in front of your body. Your hip should be bent to approximately 45 degrees and your knee bent to approximately 90 degrees.
- Hold your arms out straight in front of you with your hands clasped together. From this position, squat down until your knee is bent to approximately 60 degrees.
- Return to the start position and repeat.

TO PERFORM A SINGLE-LEG WALL SIT »

- Stand with your back against a smooth vertical wall and your feet approximately shoulder-width apart.
- Slowly slide your back down the wall until both knees and hips are at a 90-degree angle.
- Lift one foot off the ground and hold it as long as possible. After a period of rest, lift the other foot and hold it.

NOTE » If you can hold one foot up considerably longer than the other, you may need to work on developing a better balance of strength in both legs.

TO PERFORM A BROAD JUMP »

- Stand behind a line marked on the ground, with your feet slightly apart.
- Use a two-foot takeoff and landing, swinging your arms and bending your knees to provide forward drive.
- Jump as far as possible, landing on both feet without falling backwards.

NOTE » The broad jump is a great linear measurement of power in the legs.

COMPLETE ATHLETE

JOIN THE CONVERSATION!
Download the Complete Athlete app now!

UPPER-BODY STRENGTH

In Level 1, **UPPER-BODY STRENGTH** was identified as an important but overlooked aspect of fitness in soccer. But upper-body strength can be a big difference in winning balls in traffic and balance after contact. Also, upper-body strength can be an advantage for throw-ins or for goalies to get the ball accurately to defensive players.

As discussed in Level 1, pull exercises, like the bent-arm hold, are used to increase upper-back strength and mobility, while push exercises, like push-ups, increase chest and shoulder strength and mobility.

TO PERFORM A BENT-ARM HOLD PULL-UP »

- Grasp an overhead bar using an underhand grip (palms facing toward body).
- Position your body with your arms flexed and your chin clearing the bar. Your chest should be held close to the bar, with your legs hanging straight.
- Hold this position for as long as possible.

TO PERFORM PUSH-UPS »

- Lie face down on the floor (or mat) with your hands under your shoulders or slightly wider than your chest, fingers straight, legs straight and parallel.
- Straighten your arms, pushing your upper body up and keeping your back and knees straight.
- Bend your arms to lower your upper body until your elbows are at a 90-degree angle and your upper arms are parallel to the floor.
- Perform as many repetitions as possible without resting.

FLEXIBILITY / MOBILITY

A good degree of flexibility and mobility leads to better soccer technique and helps to prevent injuries. As discussed in Level 1, the sit-and-reach test is used to assess—and improve—a youth athlete's level of lower-body flexibility and mobility.

TO PERFORM THE SIT-AND-REACH TEST >>

NOTE >> You'll need a box that is 12 inches high, such as a milk crate. Tape a yardstick or ruler to the top so that the first nine inches hang over the edge and the nine-inch mark is exactly on the edge against which you will place your feet.

- Place the box against a wall.
- Sit on the floor in front of the box with your legs straight in front of you and the soles of your feet flat against the front side of the box. The overhanging part of the ruler should be pointed at your chest or midsection.
- Keeping your legs straight and flat on the floor, stretch forward and reach along the ruler with one hand on top of the other, palms down.
- Stretch forward three times without bouncing; then reach as far as possible, holding the farthest point for at least three seconds.

The purpose of the 90/90 test is to determine if the athlete has tight hamstrings and is at risk of possible leg injury. A failure in this test means you need to stretch more to gain more flexibility.

TO PERFORM A 90/90 TEST >>

- Lie on your back, legs straight and flat on the ground.
- Bend the test knee to 90 degrees and then raise it so your thigh is vertical and your knee still bent. (The non-test leg should still be straight and resting on the floor.)
- Bend at the knee to straighten your test leg. If you can extend your leg to 0 degrees (the entire leg is straight at a 90-degree angle from your body), you have passed. If you cannot straighten your leg, record what angle you have left to achieve neutral position (straight knee). Anything greater than 10 degrees is failing. (Make sure the non-test leg never bends or comes off the ground while measuring.)

CORE STRENGTH

Core strength at Level 2 continues to be important as your body grows and changes. At this level, you will be more prone to back or oblique injuries that can keep athletes off the pitch. Testing will point out any neglect to your core strength and let you know in what areas you need to improve to protect your health. **As in Level 1, we have kept the plank and med-ball throw the same, but we added the hip-lift march to test lower back, glute, and hamstring strength.**

TO PERFORM A PLANK >>

- Get down on the floor with your hands slightly wider than shoulder-width apart and your arms straight and supporting your weight.
- Make sure your body stays straight—your hips shouldn't be sticking way up in the air or sagging.
- Hold this position for as long as you can.

Overhead medicine-ball throws use the same pattern as a soccer throw-in but are a great way to measure core explosive strength in a soccer player at any age. It takes a lot of strength and coordination to throw a medicine ball.

TO PERFORM AN OVERHEAD MEDICINE-BALL THROW »

- Stand with both feet on a line, facing forward.
- Hold a medicine ball with both hands and raise it above and behind your head.
- Draw the ball back and throw it as far as possible in front of you at a 45-degree angle.
- It is ok to follow through past the line after throwing.

The **hip-lift march** helps to measure—and improve—the strength and endurance of the back muscles.

TO PERFORM A HIP-LIFT MARCH »

- Lie flat on your back with your knees bent 90 degrees and your feet flat on the ground.
- Lift your hips as high as possible, with only your shoulders and feet touching the ground.
- While keeping your hips at the same height, lift each knee in a controlled marching motion for as long as possible.

COMPLETE
ATHLETE

JOIN THE CONVERSATION!
Download the Complete Athlete app now!

SPEED / QUICKNESS / ENDURANCE

As discussed in Level 1, there are two types of soccer speed:

- Straightaway speed on an open field
- Lateral (side-to-side) quickness

The 30-yard sprint helps an athlete improve straightaway speed. The 5-10-5 shuttle run, or pro agility drill, is a great way to improve lateral quickness, because it helps to hone an athlete's ability to accelerate, decelerate, stop, and reaccelerate without losing balance. The beep test is a good way to measure and improve endurance.

TO PERFORM A 30-YARD SPRINT »

- Place two cones 30 yards apart.
- Starting at one cone, run as fast as you can to the other cone.

TO PERFORM A 5-10-5 SHUTTLE RUN »

- Set up three marker cones five yards apart.
- Start at the middle marker cone in a three-point stance.
- Turn and run five yards to the right side and touch the marker cone with your right hand.
- Turn around and run 10 yards to the left and touch the marker cone with your left hand.
- Turn and finish by running back to the middle marker cone.

TO PERFORM A BEEP TEST »

NOTE » You'll first need to download a beep test audio recording or beep test app, which will play beeps at set intervals. As the test proceeds, the interval between successive beeps reduces, forcing the athlete to increase her speed.

- Draw two lines 20 yards apart.
- Stand behind one of the line, facing the second line, and begin running when instructed by the recording.
- Continue running between the two lines, turning when signaled by the recorded beeps. After about one minute, a sound indicates an increase in speed, and the beeps will become closer together.
- The test is stopped when the athlete can no longer keep in sync with the recording.

JOIN THE CONVERSATION!
Download the Complete Athlete app now!

COMPLETE
ATHLETE

LEVEL-2 FITNESS TEST

LOWER-BODY STRENGTH »

- Single-leg squat on each leg
  for 40 seconds each
- Broad jump of 70 inches or more

UPPER-BODY STRENGTH »

- Bent-arm hold pull-up for 20 seconds
- 30 push-ups in 60 seconds

FLEXIBILITY/MOBILITY »

- Sit-and-reach test score of at least 36 centimeters
- 90/90 test is pass or fail

CORE STRENGTH/BALANCE »

- Plank for 2 $\frac{1}{2}$ minutes
- Hip-lift march with perfect form
  for 90 seconds
- Single-leg balance on each leg for 30 seconds
- Standing overhead 6-pound medicine-ball throw
  of at least 6 yards

SPEED/QUICKNESS/ENDURANCE »

- 5-10-5 shuttle run in 5.7 seconds
- 30-yard sprint in 5.0 seconds
- Beep test minimum score of 6/2-7/4 (number of
  levels/number of shuttles completed)

2.4 TECHNIQUE

In just about any sport, the basic **TECHNIQUES** are the most important skills to master. These skills are the building blocks upon which more advanced skills are learned. At Level 2, a youth soccer player needs to continue to add to the foundation of basic skills she developed in Level 1, including:

FOUNDATIONAL BALL SKILLS / DRIBBLING

PASSING

BALL-STRIKING / SHOOTING

HEADING

FOUNDATIONAL BALL SKILLS / DRIBBLING

- All surfaces of the feet
- Change of direction
- Change of pace
- Taking players on
- Keeping possession
- Creative risk-taking

TECHNICAL TIPS »

- Master the 4 cuts with inside and outside of both feet
- Maintain control of the ball
- Manipulate the ball
- Control speed with the ball
- Change speed after the cut
- Timing your cut

COMMON MISTAKES »

- Losing control of the ball
- Doing too many cuts instead of cutting and dribbling
- Timing the cut wrong
- Losing control of the ball before or after the cut
- Not using both feet

PASSING

- Passing with all surfaces of the feet
- Push pass
- Instep pass
- Outside-of-the-foot pass

- Passing by bouncing the ball off all parts of the body—chest, thighs, and head
- L-turn behind the leg
- Scissors
- Step-over

BALL-STRIKING / SHOOTING

- All surfaces
- Bending balls
- Chipping balls
- Crossing balls
- Finishing with accuracy
- Finishing with power

HEADING

- Reinforce technique
- Passing with head
- Finishing with head
- Clearing with head

**COMPLETE
ATHLETE**

JOIN THE CONVERSATION!
Download the Complete Athlete app now!

2.5 LIFESTYLE

As youth soccer players achieve higher levels of success, they will find the demands on their time increasing. Creating a healthy balance between sports, academics, family obligations, and social activities requires strong time-management skills and a clear understanding of what's important.

As a youth soccer player moves into Level 2 during the middle-school years, she should begin to develop strong organizational skills. Strong organizational skills can help her in all the following areas of her life:

FAMILY

ACADEMICS

SOCIAL LIFE

ROLE MODEL

LIVING YOUR SPORT

FAMILY

As was discussed in Level 1, parents take on a fair amount of responsibility when their daughters begin to play soccer. Parents are responsible for getting them to practices and games, both on their own and by forming carpools with other families. They help their daughters obtain and pay for equipment, uniforms, and more. And they often take time out of their busy schedules to attend games and cheer their daughters on.

Youth soccer players who develop strong organizational skills tend to have stronger, more positive family relationships. For example, youth soccer players who keep track of practice and game schedules will know when their uniforms need to be clean and won't be asking mom or dad to wash their uniforms at the last minute. Youth soccer players who keep their equipment organized and in a safe place will always know right where to find everything they need for a practice or game. Also, being aware of any regularly scheduled activities of other family members helps the youth soccer player know when her parents are available for carpooling to special practices or other events.

ACADEMICS

In addition to maintaining good grades and behaving appropriately in class, which was discussed in Level 1, a youth soccer player must remember that school is more important than sports. In fact, if a coach's decision comes down to two athletes with the same amount of athleticism, the coach will almost always choose the athlete with the better grades. In addition, higher academic achievement leads to acceptance into more colleges as well as more scholarship offers.

Middle school is obviously tougher than elementary school; nonetheless, grades must be maintained. Staying organized can go a long way toward helping a youth soccer player balance school and sports.

HOW TO STAY ORGANIZED »

- Prioritize schoolwork and make to-do lists for getting it done.
- Do what works best for your personal working style. For instance, are you good at multitasking? Or do you work best by focusing on finishing off one project at a time rather than balancing multiple tasks?

ONE LAST NOTE » Some youth soccer players consider transferring to a different high school than they're supposed to go to in order to play for a certain coach. It's far better to make sure that the high school provides a solid academic program that can help them better prepare for the SATs and for getting into the college of their choice.

COMPLETE
ATHLETE

JOIN THE CONVERSATION!
Download the Complete Athlete app now!

SOCIAL LIFE

While many youth soccer players' social lives revolve around their teammates, many have friends outside of sports. Either way, a youth soccer player should develop a lifestyle that includes spending time with friends outside of the field of play AND offline.

As was discussed in Level 1, a solid **SOCIAL LIFE** is important for all young people, not just youth athletes. The friends a young person makes can provide important support and encouragement at school and in church groups or service organizations, as well as on sports teams.

However, as girls move into middle school, cliques often emerge and can make navigating the social landscape much more difficult. It is normal for children to want to spend more time with their closest friends, but exclusionary groups can be detrimental for team growth. Parents and coaches need to keep an eye out for cliques and make sure that there is not bullying, gossip, or teasing going on. Cliques aren't confined to the field, though. Online bullying is very real; parents should carefully monitor their children's time spent on the computer and on their phones.

Spending time socializing online has become the norm for many young people. However, it's important for young people to remember that their online life isn't a substitute for spending time with friends face to face. In-person socializing provides more of the benefits of friendship and also helps youth athletes develop better interpersonal skills, which are essential for success in all areas of life.

HOW TO FIND A HEALTHY BALANCE BETWEEN ONLINE AND IN-PERSON SOCIAL INTERACTIONS >>

If you think you type more than you speak to your friends, you may need to find a healthier balance between online and in-person interactions. One way is to measure the amount of time you spend online and compare it to the amount of time you spend with your friends in person. Challenge yourself to make your in-person time greater than your online time.

PARENTS >> We stress with our players that they must turn their phones off at the start of practice and not turn them back on until practice is over. We do this to help them:

- Stay focused. If we allow them to keep their phones on, when we take a water break, they check their phones first before even rehydrating. This is, obviously, a huge distraction.
- Learn that they can live for an hour and a half without their phones. When practice is over and everyone jumps on their phones, we tease them, "What could possibly have happened in the last 90 minutes?" It's a lot like being at school; students have to have their phones put away during class. We even suggest that parents collect the phone and turn them off during dinner. This is a great way to show players how to balance appropriate times to use their phones with times when they don't need to be tethered to them.

KASSI MCCLUSKIE >> *Unfortunately, a very real issue on many girls' teams at this level is cliques. At the younger levels, everyone seems to get along and be friends, but things seem to change right around the time the players* *reach middle school and continues on into high school. It is natural for girls to have closer friendships with some members of their team than with others, but when those friendships start to turn into "alliances" or groups with "cool" and "uncool" labels, coaches and parents need to step in and nip it in the bud.*

My parents always made it a point, long before middle school, that I should befriend everyone, no matter what their social status. Everyone is different and that is what makes the world interesting; love people because of their differences! They explained that it was okay for me to have a core group of friends who I was closest to, but that I needed to pay attention to whether my group was welcoming or not welcoming. If we were closed off and kept people out, I should re-evaluate my friends. I firmly believe that my parents' insistence on this point was what helped me learn how to become a leader on my youth teams. My teammates knew that I was not going to be a part of excluding other girls or trying to turn one against another, so they felt they could trust me. I will always be grateful to my mom and dad for the deliberate effort they invested in teaching me such a valuable lesson. Now, as a coach, I encourage parents to talk to their daughters on the way home and ask specific questions, such as:

- *Whom did you pass to today?*
- *Whom have you been passing to the last couple of weeks?*
- *Have you passed to_____ lately?*
- *Have you and your friends invited someone new to be part of your warm-up group?*

Coaches also need to take action when they detect cliques starting to form among their players. I have learned not to let players pick their own teams or partners in practice, and I try always to keep mixing up the groups. If we are going on a trip, I don't have best friends room together or allow the girls to pick who rides in which van. I am always scrambling the combinations to keep anyone from forming an "us and them" mentality within our own team. That requires you to really get to know your players in order to be able to detect patterns and warning signs, but that is a great thing. Players want to know about your life, and they want you to know their favorite color and the number of brothers and sisters or pets they have. When you have a personal connection with them, there is a new level of respect, and they generally will play better all around just knowing that they are under the leadership of someone who knows them and is interested in their lives.

CAMILLE LEVIN >> When I was 13, I was part of my first national team camp—100 of us were brought in from around the country, and we were introduced to the U.S. soccer system and watched clips of Mia Hamm and other women players who were active at the time, and somehow that experience made it all click for me. My time at that camp made me decide that this was what I wanted to do and every sacrifice would be worth it. After that, I never once felt regret or feelings that I wished I was doing something else when I had to limit my time hanging out with friends or go home early from different activities in order to be ready for practice or a game.

You often hear criticisms of parents who push their children too hard to excel in sports and take it seriously, but in my case, it was actually a bit of the opposite. My *parents were incredibly supportive, but they would also sometimes tell me to relax a little or slow down a bit, because they didn't want to see me burn out. I knew what I wanted, and I had the discipline to say, "Let's go home; I need to go to bed," or "I want to stay late and practice a bit longer." I was lucky that my parents never pushed me—all my ambition and drive came from myself, and my parents supported me to make the best choices along that path.*

ROLE MODEL

At Level 1, a **ROLE MODEL** was defined as someone who possesses qualities that others admire, such as demonstrating respect for themselves and others. At Level 2, being a good role model revolves around modeling good behavior in school as well as on and off the field of play.

Good behavior starts with knowing the rules. In school, the rules usually include sitting still at your desk, listening to your teacher, and raising your hand if you want to speak. Other schools may have other rules, but generally speaking, knowing—and obeying—these rules automatically leads to good behavior.

On the field of play, good behavior starts with listening to your coaches, doing what they tell you to do, and not whining when things don't go your way. The best way to model good behavior on the field is to treat others the same way you would want them to treat you.

PARENTS >> I will always remember one girl who was a good soccer player and was also involved outside of soccer with a lot of volunteering with her family. Every weekend we did not have a game, or whenever she had some free time, she would participate in community or charity work. It was really wonderful to see, but what was even better was that she would come to practice and share stories with the other kids on our team about how good she felt about herself after helping out various causes, about interesting things that happened in the nursing homes and how they put a smile on her face— just little things that had made her day and she was excited to share. By the end of the year, three or four of her teammates had been inspired to start doing some volunteer work, too. It was really wonderful to see how one child could be a role model for the others. I think it is really important for athletes and parents alike to be open to adding some of these kinds of opportunities to the schedule. *–Ziad*

LIVING YOUR SPORT

Youth athletes who are serious about their chosen sport often cultivate a **LIFESTYLE** in which they "live" the sport. At Level 1, youth soccer players demonstrate this attribute by playing simply for the love of the game. At Level 2, youth soccer players who live for the sport spend more time practicing drills and mastering skills. These are the girls who are often seen dribbling a ball wherever and whenever they can.

They also begin to spend time watching professional women's soccer matches live or on television to learn more about the game and to see how the pros do it. Youth soccer players who live for the sport also start to spend more time learning and understanding ALL the rules of the game.

HOW TO STUDY THE RULES OF SOCCER »

The rules of soccer are based on the 17 Laws of the Game developed by Fédération Internationale de Football Association (FIFA) and maintained by the International Football Association Board (IFAB). The Laws are amended from time to time but remain largely the same from one year to the next.

To read the latest version of the Laws of the Game, go to FIFA's website at *www.FIFA.com*.

COMPLETE ATHLETE

JOIN THE CONVERSATION!
Download the Complete Athlete app now!

MIA HAMM

One of the most valuable lessons I learned about teamwork coupled with independent initiative came from the way I grew up. I was the fourth of six kids, and we all had a ton of chores or else the house would be a mess, things wouldn't get done, and we wouldn't get out the door on time. Everyone had to pitch in to make things run smoothly, and that responsibility really taught me a lot about teamwork. Because I saw it modeled effectively every day, I could understand better how those skills translated onto the soccer field.

Initiative mattered, too, because it was difficult with six kids to be able to make everyone's schedules fit together perfectly. One of my parents was usually coaching or working to help us afford to be able to play, so they weren't always available to drive us to and from practice. We had to figure out how to make it happen, whether it was riding our bikes or calling a friend and asking for a ride—we had be proactive and plan on how to meet our own responsibilities, rather than expecting our parents to keep on top of them all and drop everything to make them happen. That sense of initiative served me very well as I started to advance in the game, because I was my own source of motivation. My parents were great supporters, but they were not going to push me to practice more or work harder if I was not willing to push myself.

I think there are important lessons in that for athletes and parents alike. How do the lessons learned at home affect how you perform on the field? What do the lessons learned in sports translate to at school and at home? How does the way a parent acts at a game spill over into your personal life and relationships?

We have all seen that one parent who comes down way too hard on their child in practice or a game, yelling at them to do better, and as parents and coaches, we all resolve that we never want to be that person or allow that person to discourage our players like that. There is another aspect to consider, though, which is how you choose to express your support for your child.

When I was about 11 years old, something happened at a game that really impacted me. My dad was really involved in youth sports and often even refereed, which was great! But since there were six kids in my family, he and my mom were spread pretty thin in terms of making it to everyone's games. One day, when Dad was there as just a spectator—not a ref or anything else, he was just there to watch me play—he got really into the game and started making comments at the referees. He didn't swear or say anything terrible, but he was being loudly sarcastic, and the game was stopped so the refs could ask him to please quiet down. Eventually, they asked him to leave the sidelines, and he had to go and wait at the car until the game was over.

I will never forget how that made me feel. I was embarrassed, of course, every time I heard his voice make a crack, because everyone knew that that was my dad being mouthy. But more than that, I was so disappointed that he had to leave and wasn't able to watch me play anymore. It was such a treat to have him all to myself for a game—and then he had to leave partway through. I had to juggle both the awkwardness of having my dad get asked to leave, as well as the feelings of being let down because he wasn't able to watch me play.

At this age, games are getting more competitive, and it can really get people fired up. My dad was normally a really calm, controlled guy, but something about that game just got under his skin. Parents should try to remember that they are showing just as much support of their kids by checking their behavior at games as they are by loudly vocalizing criticism of the refs or coaches. Coaches should keep this in mind, too, and try to keep their own emotions in check, as well as encourage parents to do so.

Most children at this age aren't strong enough to say, "Mom, Dad—maybe you could show a little more restraint next time." And it's a fine line to walk, anyway, because children should be respectful of their parents and coaches, and it can be difficult to find the best way to say, "You really embarrassed me out there today with the way you were acting." The key, I think, is to make a conscious resolution ahead of time to be honestly and purposefully aware of what you say and do. That helps create a positive experience for everyone.

**COMPLETE
ATHLETE**

JOIN THE CONVERSATION!
Download the Complete Athlete
app now!

IN LEVEL 3

a soccer player has aspirations to play her best in high school with, an eye toward becoming a college soccer player. Fitness and nutrition are also taking on more importance as the sport becomes increasingly competitive. It takes more than just being a great athlete on the field, though; coaches want great students, great citizens, and great family members.

3.1 ATTITUDE

A **POSITIVE ATTITUDE** is essential to an athlete's success both on and off the playing field, especially as she moves into higher levels of play. In fact, college coaches seek out athletes who display positive attitudes.

A positive attitude is something that can be developed with practice, just like any other skill. A **COMPLETE ATHLETE** makes a habit of demonstrating the following five attributes:

RESPECT

SPORTSMANSHIP

TEAMWORK

PROFESSIONALISM

LEADERSHIP

RESPECT

Showing **RESPECT** means treating others in ways that show they have worth and value, and being considerate of other people's feelings. In Levels 1 and 2 we discussed treating coaches and players with respect. At Level 3, a youth soccer player should work on treating herself with respect.

One of the most important ways to show yourself respect is by forgiving yourself if you make a mistake in the game. Mistakes happen to everyone. The time you spend dwelling on them is time and concentration you're taking away from other areas of your life. Get over it and get right back into the game.

Respecting yourself also means taking good care of yourself physically. As a youth athlete, you need to carefully nourish and hydrate your body according to the guidelines provided in this manual, not only for optimal performance on the field of play but also for optimal health and well-being. In addition, you must not be tempted to use performance-enhancing drugs or consume alcohol or other illegal substances.

SPORTSMANSHIP

Good **SPORTSMANSHIP** starts with respect for one's teammates, opponents, coaches, and officials. At Level 3, good sportsmanship is also demonstrated by players who maintain a positive attitude when dealing with adversity.

Accountability means taking responsibility for one's own mistakes. In other words, if you make a mistake or bad play, you accept it; you do not make excuses for why it happened, and you do not blame others for it. In addition, when you know you've made a mistake, you accept the ruling on the field and do not argue with coaches or officials.

ATHLETES >> There are a couple of teams we play each year that are loaded in talent in every position—and yet we consistently outperform them. The difference-maker is sportsmanship. The whole time we play them, they are bickering back and forth and blaming one another for missing passes or failing to congratulate one another when they make them. One of the most important elements in creating a winning culture and a team that performs its best is that edge of sportsmanship. When you are on the field—and off it—you know that your coaches and teammates all love and care for one another and each person takes responsibility for his or her own role. That's one of the biggest pieces in becoming a complete athlete. *–Walid and Ziad*

COACHES >> As a coach, when I jump in on the drills with my players, playing keep-away or in a scrimmage, every time I make a bad pass or turn over the ball or miss a shot, I always tell them, "My fault, don't worry about it. My bad, my bad!" Then, when the scrimmage or drill is over, I bring the kids in and I ask, "There was one thing I did a lot—what was it?"

Immediately, the players always say, "You always said, 'My bad,' when you messed up."

"Exactly," I tell them. "I took responsibility. Some of the best sportsmanship you can demonstrate is recognizing when something is your fault."

In a game situation, when my team steps onto the field, one of the most recognizable things about them is how each player is accountable to her teammates. If a player makes a bad pass or misses a penalty kick, she says, "I'm sorry," or offers a simple gesture, like a thumbs-up. If her teammates hear or see her, they quickly say, "Don't worry about it!" It stands out so much in games because it is not only an example of great sportsmanship, but it also allows the player to feel loved by her teammates so that she doesn't have to dwell on her mistakes. She acknowledges that she didn't perform her best, but her teammates let her know she is valuable anyway. It helps everyone quickly recover emotionally from disappointments and move forward as a team. This is one of the most important habits a coach can teach his or her players. *–Ziad*

TEAMWORK

TEAMWORK means working together as a group in order to achieve a goal. In sports, players contribute their individual skills and efforts in cooperation with their teammates to win games.

By Level 3, a youth soccer player is entering high school, and the pressure may be on to maximize her playing time in order to impress college recruiters. However, a soccer player who focuses more on her own individual performance instead of the team's performance will probably not impress very many recruiters.

ATHLETES >> One of the common mistakes that players make when they are playing at a college event is to think it's all about their individual performance within a game.

For example, if a midfielder has one of her dream schools looking at her, she can often try to play more than her role. Instead of doing the usual thing she always does—one touch, two touch, keeping her teammates moving, helping defensively, helping offensively, etc.—she starts doing things she usually doesn't do, just trying to show off for the coach.

Right there, she's dropping out of her role.

Once she loses that concept, she doesn't realize how much she's hurting herself. That's one of the biggest things that I tell players over and over when we talk at half-time or after the game: You've just got to play your role and you are going to be fine. If everyone plays her role in this game, every single player is going to look her best and is going to feel very comfortable and very confident. The coach is going to see exactly what each player is doing and how she plays within the framework of the team. They will see that she knows her specific role in how she contributes to the overall success of the team. That's one of the most important things to explain to a young athlete: Play your role and let your teammates play their roles, and everyone's going to be fine. –Walid

JOIN THE CONVERSATION!
Download the Complete Athlete app now!

COMPLETE
ATHLETE

PROFESSIONALISM

Certainly a youth athlete is not a professional in the sense of being paid to play. However, developing the attitude and behaviors of a **PROFESSIONAL** can help her more easily move up through the levels.

At Level 2, a youth soccer player begins to take responsibility for keeping her uniform and equipment clean and well maintained, for maintaining her personal hygiene, and for arriving at practices and games well groomed and ready to go to work.

At Level 3, this responsibility takes on even more importance as college recruiters visit her high school to watch her team play. Players who display a professional appearance and demeanor will definitely make a good impression on recruiters.

ATHLETES >> One day, the Cal Berkeley coach called me to say he had his eye on a few players and wanted to watch them practice. I told him our practice started at 6:00 but that I show up at 5:30, so he could meet me then and we could talk before practice got started. At 5:30, I arrived and he arrived … and by 5:35, nearly every player was there, too, working on juggling or shooting or passing the ball around. At 6:00 sharp, the girls started warming up together. Every single one of them was dressed exactly how she should be, in her warm-up shirt, socks, and shoes. They were just ready to go.

The coach looked at me in surprise and said, "You told me practice starts at 6:00. Do they show up like this all the time?"

"Yes," I said. "The whole team shows up 20-30 minutes early, and they work on stuff on their own. At 6:00, we start practicing together."

"That's what I'm talking about!" he said. "Those are the types of kids I want in my program. Those are the types of kids I can win with. They look like a professional team—they act like a professional team!" I smiled at him and said, "We are a professional team. We just happen to be 15 or 16 years old." –Walid

LEADERSHIP

A good **LEADER** is able to inspire and motivate others to do something that they would not normally do, or to perform better than they would on their own. A youth soccer player can sometimes motivate and inspire her fellow players in ways that coaches cannot.

As a youth soccer player enters high school at Level 3, she should continue to develop her leadership skills through her interactions with teammates. In fact, she may decide she's ready to take her leadership skills to the next level by becoming a team leader.

A team leader needs to have the trust and respect of her teammates in order to be effective. One way to earn that trust and respect would be to encourage other players to come to her with questions, to bounce ideas off her, or even to complain. As her teammates' confidence in her grows, she can help strengthen the team through team-building and problem-solving activities.

ATHLETES >> Every time I hear the word "leadership," I think of one particular player who will always stand out to me. Carly Malatskey was absolutely a model for leadership. The girl is just unbelievable; she brings it 365 days a year, 24/7. She leads by example: never late to practice (always half an hour early, in fact); she sets up drills; she asks what the team will be doing that day; she is the first one to run after balls that go astray during shooting drills when other players are stopping to get water; and she is so positive with everyone.

Most importantly, though, although she was the most gifted player in the country (and was the #1 recruit for Stanford), she stayed humble. She was so encouraging with all the players who were less able; she was so polite to all the officials. Whenever people asked me what was special about that group, I always said, "I have a great team, and I have an unbelievable leader."

We were in a game where, as one of the final four, all we had to do was win to qualify for the national championship final game. We were up 3-2 when the referee added six minutes of stoppage time, and we maintained that lead for five minutes and fifty seconds. Then, in the last ten seconds of the stoppage time, the other team scored to tie the game and then bumped us out on the goal differential to qualify for the national championship game.

I can't tell you how hard it was for me, as a coach, to watch that moment. Can you imagine how the players felt? The referee whistled the end of the game and a lot of the players went down, crying, on their knees, absolutely crushed. After the commitment and sacrifices they went through all year to get to that point, they were literally ten seconds away from making a national championship final—and it slips away.

As I was looking at that scene of the girls sunk on the field crushed and the girls on the bench crying, one person was standing up, holding herself together. Carly was reaching out to the other players, lifting them back up to their feet, hugging them, telling them it's okay. That was one of her shining moments as a leader for the team. Here they were in their lowest moment, and yet she continued to encourage and support her teammates.

The Stanford coach happened to be at that game and he noticed her incredible leadership, too. He said, "I love that kid." I said I did, too. He just shook his head and said, "What a leader. What a leader."

That's what is so important to remember: Select team coaches, college coaches, professional coaches—they are all looking for leaders. –*Ziad*

KASSI MCCLUSKIE » *Persistence is so important. Year after year after year, I was on a team that would travel out to California for the Surf Cup and get beaten terribly: 6-0 one year, 5-0 the next. It was painful. But we kept going because we knew that the only way to get better was to keep pushing ourselves by playing "up" against teams that were better than us, rather than playing teams we knew we could beat easily. Finally, in our fifth year, and after gradually getting better each year, we finally won the entire tournament my sophomore year of high school. It is still one of my favorite and most memorable wins because we had fought through the disappointment and discouragement for so long and had just kept fighting and improving and closing the gap until we finally came out on top!*

COMPLETE ATHLETE

JOIN THE CONVERSATION!
Download the Complete Athlete app now!

3.2 PREPARATION

As we discussed in Levels 1 and 2, **PREPARATION** refers to off-the-field activities, such as practicing skills, eating right, staying hydrated, getting enough rest, and mentally preparing for a game or practice. Coaches love athletes who prepare: These are the players who are eager to learn, eager to play, and, ultimately, eager to win. They are the athletes that coaches want to help succeed, because they already have a winning attitude. Preparation also helps athletes feel positive and confident in their ability to perform.

A **COMPLETE ATHLETE** prepares to perform on the field of play by continuously improving on the following:

PRACTICE

NUTRITION

HYDRATION

RECOVERY

MENTALITY

PRACTICE

A youth athlete who has surpassed Level 2 obviously considers soccer a huge part of her life. By this point, she should have already begun to work with a private soccer coach to master the basic techniques and to begin to learn a few position-specific skills.

At Level 3, a youth athlete should begin to identify those positions at which she is most proficient. Both her team soccer coaches as well as her private coach can help her decide which positions make the most sense for her. In addition to team **PRACTICES** and one-on-one sessions with her private coach, the youth soccer player can continue her regular individual practice sessions, focusing extra attention on the skills needed for the positions she wants to play.

ONE ADDITIONAL NOTE >> College coaches look for—and recruit—the players who are contributing the most. The more proficient a player is at more positions, the more game time she will get.

COACHES >> When I took a team to Virginia to play in the Jefferson Cup, we were invited to visit the University of Virginia's soccer facility by coach Steve Swanson, one of the top coaches in the country and assistant coach on the women's national team. He showed us around and when we reached the locker room, I noticed a board covered with numbers. I asked him what it was about and he explained that after each practice, he has his players rate themselves, on a scale of 1 to 10, how they practiced as a team and then how they did individually.

That made a big impact on me, and I brought the idea home to implement with my teams. I tell my players that before they come to practice, they need to write down certain things that we need to accomplish. Then, on the back of that sheet of paper, they should start grading themselves and their practice. If they keep that sheet in the car and look at it before and after each practice, they can keep track over a month of how well they did.

For example, if a forward is working on shooting and makes five shots out of ten, she should write that down. At the next practice, she should aim to do one better; the practice after that, even better. It provides a way for the players to measure their success and also really to focus on beating the previous day's grade. It elevates individual practice to a new level.

As a team, I have them discuss practice and go over how they are doing as a group while they cool down. How well did they work together? How much effort did they seem to invest in the practice as a unit? How well did they execute their drills and improve their skills? I have them come up with a rating so that they are grading themselves as a team, too. I think it is a really fantastic system and I credit Coach Swanson for such a great idea!
—*Walid*

JOIN THE CONVERSATION!
Download the Complete Athlete app now!

COMPLETE
ATHLETE

NUTRITION

As a youth soccer player enters high school, **NUTRITION** continues to play a key role in her life. Nutrition is important not only for optimal performance on the field of play, but also to obtain the vitamins and minerals she needs for optimal health.

LEVEL-3 ATHLETE NUTRITION GUIDELINES »

Each individual has different macronutrient needs, based on height, weight, age, activity level, and genetic background. The following macronutrient guidelines are based on age and estimated activity level for a Level-3 athlete:

- 50% carbohydrate
- 25% protein
- 25% fat
- No more than 7% saturated fat
- No trans fat
- 38 grams of fiber per day
- No more than 150 calories per day from sugar (37.5 grams or 9 teaspoons)

COACHES » When athletes get into high school, nutrition continues to play a key role. When I was coaching for Newport Harbor High School, I noticed a huge difference in the energy level of the kids practicing right after school and playing games on weeknights, as opposed to the club schedule, where practice was in the evening and games were on weekends. I was so confused, because it seemed like the Newport Harbor athletes were not playing nearly to their best level. When I asked them about their eating habits, it all made sense.

They were having junk-food lunches during the day, and this was the last meal they ate before practice or games after school. I stressed to them that they had to give their bodies the fuel necessary to power them through practice and games.

Coaches need to continually remind players that it is vitally important to put the right nutrition in their bodies for them to have that great performance. Athletes at Level 3 need to start thinking about nutrition as an element in the overall plan to grow stronger and faster.
–*Ziad*

HYDRATION

If an athlete does not drink enough water, she could suffer from dehydration. Warning signs of dehydration include:

- Thirst
- Irritability
- Headache
- Weakness
- Dizziness
- Cramps
- Nausea
- Increased risk of injury

HOW TO MAINTAIN PROPER HYDRATION*>>

- Before exercise, drink 16-20 full ounces within the 2-hour period prior to exercise.
- During exercise, drink 4-6 full ounces.
- After exercise, replace 24 full ounces for every one pound of body weight lost during exercise.
* *Adapted from guidelines provided by the American College of Sports Medicine (ACSM)*

ATHLETES >> I cannot stress enough the importance of hydration. A few years ago, we took a team to a college showcase called the Texas Shootout. Our players are all from Southern California and were not used to the heat and humidity, so despite our urging them to hydrate as much as possible, not everyone took the warning seriously.

One of the players had not had nearly enough water ahead of time and even though she absolutely dominated in the first half, she began cramping badly in the second half. We eventually had to pull her and put another player in. As it turned out, a college coach had come specifically to watch her play ... but he had only come for the second half of the game. It was such a waste of an opportunity.

I cannot stress enough how important it is to maintain proper nutrition—of which hydration is a major component—because it really has a direct impact on performance. And the fact is, college coaches could be at any game, not just a showcase. The high-school season runs during their off-season, so they can show up at any time. You've absolutely got to take care of your body, make sure you're hydrated right, and be ready to perform! *–Walid*

RECOVERY

Youth soccer players need to eat and drink within 30 minutes of a practice or game to make up for the calories they are burning and fluids they are using. Replenishing calories and fluids also aids in muscle recovery and repair.

HOW TO REPLENISH CALORIES AND FLUIDS >>

- Drink 24 ounces of fluid for every pound of sweat lost within a 2-hour period of a game or practice.
- Consume 20-25 grams of protein plus an equal amount of carbohydrates within the 30-minute recovery window.

JOIN THE CONVERSATION!
Download the Complete Athlete app now!

COMPLETE
ATHLETE

SLEEP An athlete's body does its growing, healing, and muscle repair during sleep. A high-school–aged athlete may still be going through a growth spurt; therefore, sleep is crucial for proper growth and development. According to the National Sleep Foundation, a Level-3 youth athlete should get 8-10 hours of sleep each night for proper growth and development.

A lot of youth soccer players stress out about the amount of sleep they may be getting, especially the night before a big game. It's best not to put too much emphasis on the quality of your sleep the night before game day, because the anticipation and excitement can cause restless sleep. Instead, consider the most important night of sleep to be two days before game day, and the second most important night of sleep to be three days before game day. Make sure you get the sleep you need on those nights, and try to rest up before the actual game on game day.

COACHES » As athletes get older and the games get more intense, they need to focus even more on stretching and taking care of their muscles. One thing that my teams have started doing is that when we travel, we fill up a bathtub in the hotel with ice and the girls take turns using the ice bath to soothe their muscles after a game. If there is no bathtub in the rooms, we buy a big trash can and fill it with ice, and the players take turns going in.

I also make sure that the players take a walk after breakfast and stretch afterward. These are little things, but they help our players feel confident and mentally more prepared; most importantly, though, it helps those muscles recover for the next game. *–Walid*

MENTALITY

Being a better athlete does not necessarily mean training harder or longer. Certainly a youth soccer player must spend time physically preparing her body to meet the demands of a practice session or game. Similarly, engaging in **MENTAL PREPARATION** can help her perform at a higher level by creating the proper mindset for either practice or a game.

To be successful in any sport, athletes must apply 100 percent of their energy and thoughts toward each activity. In other words, they need to have their "heads in the game." At Level 3, youth soccer players should work on staying focused.

HOW TO IMPROVE YOUR FOCUS >>

The following suggestions are adapted from *Sports Psychology For Dummies* by Leif H. Smith and Todd M. Kays.

KNOW WHAT YOU NEED TO FOCUS ON. The clearer you are about what you need to focus on, the more likely you'll be to stay focused on the factors that contribute to your success.

FOCUS ON WHAT YOU CAN CONTROL. You have control over yourself and your own actions and attitudes—nothing more. Keep your focus here. If you focus on outcomes (things you have no control over), you're creating unnecessary anxiety. Focus on the process and you increase the likelihood of positive results happening.

STAY RELAXED UNDER PRESSURE. When you're stressed and anxious, your focus drops. Find ways to stay calm in high-pressure situations, such as taking deep breaths, stretching muscles to loosen them, or engaging in effective routines to keep your focus where it needs to be.

USE CUE WORDS. Cue words are simple words and phrases that remind you of your focus points. Repeating words and phrases such as *relax, play hard,* or *quick feet* will remind you to focus on what you need to do. If your mind is focused on your cue words, your body will follow.

COACHES » I had a team that was playing to qualify for the national finals in Colorado, but the game was postponed a day due to thunderstorms ... and then was postponed again. We had to change our flights, make sure we could secure our hotel rooms for another night—there was just so much to deal with. But the most important thing for me was making sure that the players were mentally prepared for the game.

I called a team meeting and had everyone step up and talk about their experience with the team and what the upcoming game meant and how it was going to give these girls, who were all juniors and seniors in high school, one last event and trip together as a team. I was trying to bring their mentality back to the game from the chaos of the disrupted travel plans. That was my motive, and it worked. The shift in focus was obvious. It helped the whole team center their minds on where they needed to be.

We had one girl who had injured her ankle—it was absolutely swollen—but Kayla Mills (who went on to play for the University of Southern California and become the Pac-12 Defensive Player of the Year and who is now playing internationally), looked at her injured teammate and said, "You're going to be ready to play tomorrow."

The girl immediately answered, "I'm playing." You could just feel the mentality in the room shifting as they all turned their focus toward the game.

When it was my turn to speak, I just told them all how much I loved them and how proud I was of them. Then I added, "When you sleep tonight, I want you to dream about that goal you are going to score, about that tackle you are going to make, about that save you are going to make." Now that they had that laser-focus as a team, I wanted them to switch to thinking individually about how each person has to play her own part to make the team function as a whole. It really was an incredibly difficult match-up, and a tie wouldn't be enough to get us into the finals; we had to win outright. Ziad called me that night and said, "Man, it's going to be a tough game." I told him, "We already won that game. The game is over with. Tomorrow is just a formality." Sure enough, we won 3-1. Those girls just had their mentality exactly where it needed to be, thanks to the incredible energy and focus they managed despite all the stressors of the night before. –Walid

KASSI MCCLUSKIE >> *When I was in high school, my team was in the regional finals, and right at the end of the game, I ended up scoring on my own team. We lost because of how I messed up a pass.*

I beat myself up so badly over that, because I believed everything was my fault, so feeling awful was the right

way to feel in that situation. Eventually, however, I came to realize that I had to find a balance. Yes, it was crushing and I should care enough to feel disappointed, take responsibility, and own up to my mistakes. But I also needed to recognize that I had been an integral part of my team's success up to that point. My teammates were amazingly gracious and would reassure me, saying, "We wouldn't have even gotten this far if it wasn't for you being a part of our team"—and I finally realized that I needed to accept what they were saying and let that be part of my healing.

Mistakes are going to happen. Usually they will be pretty small, but occasionally they will be huge. If that's the case, it's okay to be mad about it! In fact, that is healthy because it shows you take things seriously; but also allow yourself to let go and move forward. That's the only way you're going to get better and learn from it.

CAMILLE LEVIN » *The best advice I can offer an athlete in trying to find the right "fit" with a soccer program and coach is to look for a good balance. You want a coach who shows confidence in you and believes in you, but who will also push you the right amount to keep growing. The ultimate issue is whether or not your coach is supportive of you and your development. Winning is important, of course, but you need to look for a team that offers you more than just a lot of wins.*

It all depends on the individual. Some people respond better to one type of coaching personality and some to another. Just be honest about what way works best for you and then seek out a coach who manages the team in that way and makes you feel valued as well as challenged.

3.3 FITNESS

FITNESS matters. Strength and speed are required to play the game of soccer effectively. Flexibility and mobility help to prevent injuries. As a youth soccer player reaches Level 3, she can separate herself from other players by demonstrating a serious dedication to her own personal fitness. Not only does this help to establish a foundation of strength; it also teaches good habits needed for success in higher levels of soccer. After all, the demands of training at the college and pro levels can be mentally and physically challenging, especially for those athletes who are not already used to working that hard at lower levels of the sport in the following areas:

LOWER-BODY STRENGTH

UPPER-BODY STRENGTH

FLEXIBILITY / MOBILITY

CORE STRENGTH

SPEED / QUICKNESS / ENDURANCE

LOWER-BODY STRENGTH

The demands to your fitness and health during practice and games can depend on how strong you are in your legs. We know stronger legs can make you faster to the point of contact, but they can also allow you to out-jump your opponent for free balls in the air or win slide tackles. Strong and fit lower bodies are the foundation of staying healthy and being able to absorb the pounding of tough practices or long seasons. You will still be tested and should show improvement with the single-leg squat and broad jump, but we have added the vertical test now, which will measure how powerful your legs are to jump up high. Your strength in jumping is a major test colleges will want to see. When an athlete has equal strength in both legs, she will produce higher scores.

TO PERFORM SINGLE-LEG SQUATS >>

- Stand on one leg while your other leg is lifted off the ground in front of your body. Your hip should be bent to approximately 45 degrees and your knee bent to approximately 90 degrees.
- Hold your arms out straight in front of you with the hands clasped together. From this position, squat down until your knee is bent to approximately 60 degrees.
- Return to the start position and repeat.

TO PERFORM A SINGLE-LEG WALL SIT >>

- Stand with your back against a smooth vertical wall and your feet approximately shoulder-width apart.
- Slowly slide your back down the wall until both knees and hips are at a 90-degree angle.

- Lift one foot off the ground and hold it as long as possible. After a period of rest, lift the other foot and hold it.

  NOTE >> If you can hold one foot up considerably longer than the other, you may need to work on developing a better balance of strength in both legs.

TO PERFORM A BROAD JUMP >>

- Stand behind a line marked on the ground, with your feet slightly apart.
- Use a two-foot takeoff and landing, swinging your arms and bending your knees to provide forward drive.
- Jump as far as possible, landing on both feet without falling backward.

  NOTE >> Broad jump is a great linear measurement of power in the legs.

TO PERFORM A VERTICAL JUMP TEST >>

- Stand next to any wall and, with your feet completely flat, reach up with your hand closest to the wall and measure the highest point you can touch. (This is easier to do with two people so the other person can mark and measure.)
- With your arm still raised, jump as high as you can and note how high you are able to touch.
- Measure the distance between the two points for your vertical jump score.

UPPER-BODY STRENGTH

Girls are older and players are getting stronger. You need to stay ahead of the curve to make sure you can win balls and keep from getting bounced off better and stronger opponents. In order to do well at these tests and to keep seeing improvement, you need to get in the weight room and put emphasis on upper-body exercises. In the highly competitive levels like high school and club ball, girls will be more aggressive; having that extra strength in your upper body will allow you to absorb contact better and not lose balance—or worse, lose the ball!

TO PERFORM A VERTICAL PULL-UP »

- Grasp an overhead bar using the neutral grip or underhand grip (palms facing toward body), with your arms fully extended and your legs hanging straight down.
- Raise your body up until your chin clears the top of the bar.
- Lower again to the starting position, with your arms fully extended.

TO PERFORM PUSH-UPS »

- Lie face down on the floor (or mat) with your hands under your shoulders or slightly wider than your chest, fingers straight, legs straight and parallel.
- Straighten your arms, pushing your upper body up and keeping your back and knees straight.
- Bend your arms to lower your upper body until your elbows are at a 90-degree angle and your upper arms are parallel to the floor.
- Perform as many repetitions as possible without resting.

TO PERFORM AN OVERHEAD MEDICINE-BALL THROW »

- Stand with both feet on a line, facing forward.
- Hold a medicine ball with both hands and raise it above and behind your head.
- Draw the ball back and throw it as far as possible in front of you at a 45-degree angle.
- It is okay to follow through past the line after throwing.

FLEXIBILITY / MOBILITY

A good degree of **FLEXIBILITY** and **MOBILITY** leads to better soccer technique and helps to prevent injuries. As discussed in Levels 1 and 2, the sit-and-reach test is used to assess—and improve—a youth athlete's level of lower-body flexibility and mobility. Likewise, the sit-and-reach test is used to assess—and improve—a youth athlete's level of upper-body flexibility and mobility.

TO PERFORM THE SIT-AND-REACH TEST »

NOTE » You'll need a box that is 12 inches high, such as a milk crate. Tape a yardstick or ruler to the top so that the first 9 inches hang over the edge and the 9-inch mark is exactly on the edge against which you will place your feet.

- Place the box against a wall.
- Sit on the floor in front of the box with your legs straight in front of you and the soles of your feet flat against the front side of the box. The overhanging part of the ruler should be pointed at your chest or midsection.
- Keeping your legs straight and flat on the floor, stretch forward and reach along the ruler with one hand on top of the other, palms down.
- Stretch forward three times without bouncing; then reach as far as possible, holding the farthest point for at least three seconds.

The purpose of the 90/90 test is to determine if the athlete has tight hamstrings and is at risk of possible leg injury. A failure in this test means you need to stretch more to gain more flexibility.

TO PERFORM A 90/90 TEST ≫

- Lie on your back, legs straight and flat on the ground.
- Bend the test knee to 90 degrees and then raise it so your thigh is vertical and your knee still bent. (The non-test leg should still be straight and resting on the floor.)
- Bend at the knee to straighten your test leg. If you can extend your leg to 0 degrees (the entire leg is straight at a 90-degree angle from your body), you have passed. If you cannot straighten your leg, record what angle you have left to achieve neutral position (straight knee). Anything greater than 10 degrees is failing. (Make sure the non-test leg never bends or comes off the ground while measuring.)

CORE STRENGTH

Building up core strength for an athlete competing in top club teams or trying to break into the starting lineup for high school can be the game-changer. Don't forget that the core is the glue for all the hard work you have been doing in the gym training your whole body for athletic success. It allows the larger muscles to convert energy into whatever athletic move you are going to make, be it kicking a ball or dodging an opponent.

COMPLETE ATHLETE

JOIN THE CONVERSATION!
Download the Complete Athlete app now!

TO PERFORM A PLANK >>

- Get down on the floor with your hands slightly wider than shoulder-width apart and your arms straight and supporting your weight.
- Make sure your body stays straight—your hips shouldn't be sticking way up in the air or sagging.
- Hold this position for as long as you can.

TO PERFORM A SIDE PLANK >>

- Lie on your side with your legs straight.
- Prop your upper body up on your elbow and forearm. Make sure your elbow is aligned with your shoulder.
- Brace your core by contracting your abs forcefully and then raise your hips until your body forms a straight line from your ankles to your shoulders.
- Breathe deeply while holding this position.
- Repeat this exercise on your other side.

The **hip-lift march** helps to measure—and improve—the strength and endurance of your back muscles.

TO PERFORM A HIP-LIFT MARCH >>

- Lie flat on your back with your knees bent 90 degrees and your feet flat on the ground.
- Lift your hips as high as possible, with only your shoulders and feet touching the ground.
- While keeping your hips at the same height, lift each knee in a controlled marching motion for as long as possible.

SPEED / QUICKNESS / ENDURANCE

As discussed in Levels 1 and 2, there are two types of soccer speed:

- Straightaway speed on an open field
- Lateral (side-to-side) quickness

The 30-yard sprint helps an athlete improve straightaway speed. The 5-10-5 shuttle run, or pro agility drill, is a great way to improve lateral quickness, because it helps to hone an athlete's ability to accelerate, decelerate, stop, and reaccelerate without losing balance. The beep test is a good way to measure and improve endurance.

TO PERFORM A 30-YARD SPRINT »

- Place two cones 30 yards apart.
- Starting at one cone, run as fast as you can to the other cone.

TO PERFORM A 5-10-5 SHUTTLE RUN »

- Set up three marker cones five yards apart.
- Start at the middle marker cone in a three-point stance.
- Turn and run five yards to the right side and touch the marker cone with your right hand.
- Turn around and run 10 yards to the left and touch the marker cone with your left hand.
- Turn and finish by running back to the middle marker cone.

COMPLETE ATHLETE

JOIN THE CONVERSATION!
Download the Complete Athlete app now!

TO PERFORM A BEEP TEST >>

NOTE >> You'll first need to download a beep test audio recording or beep test app, which will play beeps at set intervals. As the test proceeds, the interval between successive beeps reduces, forcing the athlete to increase her speed.

- Draw two lines 40 yards apart.
- Stand behind one of the lines, facing the second line, and begin running when instructed by the recording.
- Continue running between the two lines, turning when signaled by the recorded beeps. After about one minute, a sound indicates an increase in speed, and the beeps will become closer together.
- The test is stopped when the athlete can no longer keep in sync with the recording.

LEVEL-3 FITNESS TEST

LOWER-BODY STRENGTH »

- 8 full-range single-leg squats on each leg
- Single-leg wall squat for at least 60 seconds
- Broad jump of 78 inches or more
- Vertical jump of 17 inches or more

UPPER-BODY STRENGTH »

- Bent-arm, hold pull-up for 25 seconds
- 35 push-ups in 60 seconds

FLEXIBILITY/MOBILITY »

- Sit-and-reach test score of at least 38 centimeters
- 90/90 test is pass or fail

CORE STRENGTH/BALANCE »

- Plank for $2 \frac{1}{2}$ minutes
- Side plank for 40 seconds on each side
- Hip-lift march with perfect form for 2 minutes
- Single-leg balance on each leg for 30 seconds
- Standing overhead 6-pound medicine-ball throw for at least 7 yards

SPEED/QUICKNESS/ENDURANCE »

- 5-10-5 shuttle run in 5.3 seconds
- 30-yard sprint in 4.7 seconds
- Beep test minimum score of 6/9–8/2 (number of levels/ number of shuttles completed)

3.4 TECHNIQUE

In just about any sport, the basic **TECHNIQUES** are the most important skills to master. These skills are the building blocks upon which more advanced skills are learned. Although you might have started to specialize in a specific position at Level 2, in Level 3 you will spend the majority of your private practice time in the position you (or your coaches) feel you will play at the next level. If you're serious about succeeding at higher levels of soccer, professional instruction is highly recommended.

Remember, a **COMPLETE ATHLETE** not only masters the basic and advanced skills needed to play the game of soccer, but she also understands the roles and responsibilities of every position on a team and how all the positions work together to win games. The basic skills of soccer include:

FOUNDATIONAL BALL SKILLS / DRIBBLING

PASSING

BALL CONTROL

BALL STRIKING / SHOOTING

HEADING

FOUNDATIONAL BALL SKILLS / DRIBBLING

- Refine and combine
- Consistent solid moves go to 4-5, to go to with emphasis on both feet
- Everything is at game-related speed
- Creative risk-taking
- Quick change of direction
- Change of speed/pace

PASSING

- Refine passing with all surfaces of the feet
- Efficient passing with all parts of the body
- Accuracy with short, medium, and long passes
- Deception with ones passing ability
- Ability to read where and when to pass the ball before receiving the ball
- Ability to think ahead and read the passing options first, second, or third
- Consistency in the weight and texture of all passes

BALL CONTROL

- All surfaces of the feet and body
- Reading and receiving away from pressure
- First touch with purpose
- Change of speed with turns
- Turning on the move
- Turning to pass
- Turning to finish

BALL-STRIKING / SHOOTING

- Bending balls
- Chipping
- Finishing with power and accuracy
- Flighted balls driven and lofted
- Inside of the foot
- Outside of the foot
- Instep
- Volley instep and inside foot

HEADING

- For direction to flick
- To teammate
- To defend
- To score

3.5 LIFESTYLE

As youth soccer players achieve higher levels of success, they will find the demands on their time increasing. Creating a healthy balance between sports, academics, family obligations, and social activities requires strong time-management skills and a clear understanding of what's important.

As a youth soccer player moves into Level 3 during the high school years, the way she balances the following elements in her life will shift as she and her family begin to focus on getting into college and earning scholarships:

FAMILY

ACADEMICS

SOCIAL LIFE AND ROLE MODEL

LIVING YOUR SPORT

FAMILY

College coaches want mature, respectful student-athletes as part of their program. Many observe how prospects treat their parents when they visit the school. Youth soccer players who have worked hard to maintain positive relationships with their families will definitely stand out.

In Levels 1 and 2, a youth soccer player's parents take on a fair amount of responsibility. At Level 3, parents are probably spending a great deal more money for soccer, in terms of better equipment, private coaching sessions, and more. They are also likely devoting even more of their time to support their daughter's desire to excel in soccer.

As a youth soccer player moves into more serious levels of play, she should begin to assume more of the responsibility for soccer activities. This helps the youth soccer player learn to be independent and self-sufficient, two traits that she will need to succeed in college.

HOW TO BECOME MORE INDEPENDENT AND SELF-SUFFICIENT >>

- Always remember all that your parents do to support you. Be grateful. NEVER take your parents for granted.
- Try to be helpful around the house. At the very least, keep your room clean and pick up after yourself.
- Always have your equipment well organized. Your parents should never have to nag you about getting ready for games and practices.

- Once you earn a driver's license, drive yourself to practices.
- If you're exhausted or sore from soccer, do something about it; don't whine to everyone or walk around in a bad mood. Take a nap if you're tired. To relieve sore muscles, try taking a bath with Epsom salts.

ATHLETES AND PARENTS >> The most common questions I get asked when I get a phone call from a collegiate coach are: How is the player? How is she as a person? How is her lifestyle? Can you talk to me about her parents?

What is important for players and parents both to realize is that not every kid out there is a blue chip. When coaches make their home visits and meet with the player and her family—or even just talk with her after a game—the coach is looking at a dozen other players at the same level in terms of both talent and academics. The difference-maker is, very often, whether the player showed respect to her parents and the way the parents represented themselves in that brief moment in which the coach encountered them. Are the parents going to be an absolute nightmare to deal with? And, more importantly, does the athlete show respect to her parents, or was she cutting them off, ordering them around, and just being rude? If a player doesn't have respect for her parents, how can she have respect for her coach? It is really important that athletes realize that coaches are looking for that. At the end of the day, that coach is going to have that player for four years—five, if she red-shirts. Coaches want a player who is a **COMPLETE ATHLETE**, shows respect, and has parents who are going to be supportive.

—Ziad

ACADEMICS

Throughout Levels 1 and 2, a youth soccer player should have been laying the foundation for strong academic achievement. Level 3 is the time for developing plans for getting into college and earning scholarships.

WHERE TO FIND ANSWERS REGARDING COLLEGE ATHLETICS »

The National Collegiate Athletic Association, or NCAA (*www.ncaa.org*), serves as the athletics governing body for more than 1,300 colleges, universities, conferences, and organizations. The organization has a wide range of resources available to help youth soccer players and their parents understand the eligibility requirements for earning scholarships and playing sports at the college level, including:

- NCAA Guide for the College-Bound Student-Athlete, which is available as a free download from the www.ncaa.org website
- The NCAA Eligibility Center's resource page on its website. Go to *www.eligibilitycenter.org* and click on "Resources."
- *www.ncaa.org/student-athletes/future*

COMPLETE ATHLETE

JOIN THE CONVERSATION!
Download the Complete Athlete app now!

UNDERSTANDING SCHOLARSHIPS AND ELIGIBILITY TO PLAY »

Each NCAA Division has different scholarship opportunities and eligibility requirements. For example, only NCAA Divisions-I and -II colleges and universities award athletics scholarships. Division-III colleges and universities do not award athletics scholarships, but they do provide academic scholarships as well as need-based financial aid.

ELIGIBILITY TO PLAY FOR A DIVISION-I COLLEGE OR UNIVERSITY* »

According to the NCAA website, to be eligible to play at a Division-I college or university, a youth soccer player must:

COMPLETE 16 CORE COURSES, finishing at least 10 of them before the seventh semester, with at least seven of them in English, math, or natural science.

EARN AT LEAST A 2.3 GPA IN THE CORE COURSES.

EARN AN SAT OR ACT SCORE MATCHING YOUR CORE-COURSE GPA ON THE DIVISION-I SLIDING SCALE. The sliding-scale balances your test score with your GPA. If you have a low test score, you need a higher GPA to be eligible. If you have a low GPA, you need a higher test score to be eligible.

REGISTER WITH THE NCAA ELIGIBILITY CENTER to ensure you meet the NCAA amateurism standards and are academically prepared for college coursework. The NCAA Eligibility Center certifies the initial academic eligibility and amateur status of all college-bound student-athletes who wish to compete in NCAA Division-I or -II athletics.

These eligibility guidelines are for students enrolling full-time at a Division-I school after August 1, 2016.

ELIGIBILITY TO PLAY FOR A DIVISION-II COLLEGE OR UNIVERSITY* >>

According to the NCAA website, to be eligible to play at a Division-II college or university, a youth soccer player must:

COMPLETE 16 CORE COURSES, finishing at least 10 of them before the seventh semester, with at least seven of them in English, math, or natural science.

EARN AT LEAST A 2.2 GPA IN THE CORE COURSES.

EARN AN SAT OR ACT SCORE MATCHING YOUR CORE-COURSE GPA ON THE DIVISION-II SLIDING SCALE. The sliding scale balances your test score with your GPA. If you have a low test score, you need a higher GPA to be eligible. If you have a low GPA, you need a higher test score to be eligible.

REGISTER WITH THE NCAA ELIGIBILITY CENTER to ensure you meet the NCAA amateurism standards and are academically prepared for college coursework. The NCAA Eligibility Center certifies the initial academic eligibility and amateur status of all college-bound student-athletes who wish to compete in NCAA Division-I or -II athletics.

* *These eligibility guidelines are for students enrolling full-time at a Division-II school after August 1, 2016.*

While Division-III schools do not offer athletics scholarships, 75 percent of Division-III student-athletes receive some form of merit or need-based financial aid. If you are planning to attend a Division-III school, you do not need to register with the NCAA Eligibility Center. Division-III schools set their own admissions standards. For more information about Division-III schools, go to *www.ncaa.org/d3* or visit the websites of the schools you're most interested in attending.

IMPORTANT STRATEGIES >>

- Visit *www.eligibilitycenter.org* to learn more about opportunities available at NCAA colleges and universities.
- Spend time with your family researching colleges. Learn what your colleges or universities of choice look for in a student-athlete, and be realistic about your ability to succeed.
- Consult with your school counselor throughout high school to ensure you are on track to graduate having completed all required NCAA-approved core courses.
- Plan to take the PSAT exam in your sophomore year to get an idea of how you might do on the SAT exam.
- Plan to take the SAT and ACT exams a few times. The higher your score on these exams, the more scholarship money will be available to you at any of the NCAA colleges or universities.
- Maintain your grades and graduate on time.

ATHLETES » It is very important that students start to focus on their grades beginning in their freshman year. Sometimes a player will think, "I don't really need to worry until my junior year because colleges will just look at my grades as an upperclassman and my SATs. I'll be fine." But the reality is that colleges look at all of a student's transcripts, and it just might be that that bad grade from your freshman or sophomore year comes back to haunt you.

PARENTS AND COACHES » There are a lot of kids who have natural talent on the field and are going to be scouted by every major coach because they are such standout players. But especially if athletes want to go to Ivy League or Pac-12 schools or schools in some of the other major conferences, they need to have a very clear sense of the academic requirements. Work with your kids to understand what their scores need to look like. Spend time researching each school's policies, minimum SAT scores, average GPA, etc.

Sports can take you up to a point, but the academic side is what will set a player apart—good or bad—from other athletes with similar talent and potential. Figuring out early on which schools are a good fit for your player, or what degree of academic rigor she does or does not want can help you decide together on which schools to really focus your collective energies.

CAMILLE LEVIN » *When it comes to choosing a college, you need to choose the right school for you. Hopefully, you will have several options to consider, but listen to your gut as to which one is really the best fit. I looked at a number of really phenomenal programs that would allow a player to give a verbal commitment* *before you were actually admitted to the college itself. I had a lot of friends, who as sophomores in high school, were doing just that. That was the right choice for them. For me, I wasn't ready at that point to make a decision and, anyway, I wanted to see if I could get into Stanford academically. But Stanford won't allow a commitment until you have already been accepted.*

So I waited until early in my senior year and applied to Stanford, but I continued to build relationships with the other coaches until I heard that I'd gotten in. Then I went ahead and made the commitment to play for Stanford. That may not be the right path for everyone but, for me, it was worth waiting the extra year or two to commit because the program seemed like the right place for me to be.

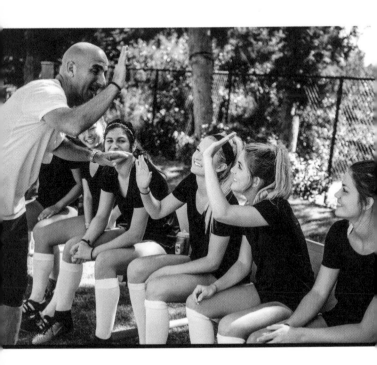

SOCIAL LIFE AND ROLE MODEL

At Level 3, a youth soccer player's **SOCIAL LIFE** may take a back seat to academics and sports. However, maintaining positive relationships with friends is still very important. Young people who maintain strong friendships tend to be happier and more successful in school as well as on the field.

At this point in a youth soccer player's life, her closest friends may be fellow soccer players, because these are the people she spends most of her time with. These are also the people she has the most in common with. The truth is, many lifelong friendships are formed between youth athletes who play the same sport. However, lifelong friendships are usually only developed by people who know how to recognize—and be—a true friend.

HOW TO RECOGNIZE—AND BE—A TRUE FRIEND »

BE TRUSTWORTHY. True friends earn trust by always having each other's back and never sharing anything that was said in confidence.

SHARE VALUES. True friends share many of the same values, such as getting good grades or playing fair.

BE EMPATHETIC. True friends are happy for each other when good things happen and sympathetic when bad things happen.

CONTINUE TO BE A GOOD ROLE MODEL. Model good behavior by staying away from illegal drugs, alcohol, tobacco, and performance-enhancing substances, and by avoiding other risky behaviors.

AGREE TO DISAGREE. Friendships are tested when disagreements occur, but true friends work to move past the disagreements and don't abandon the friendship because of them.

Sometime friendships do end because of disagreements. For instance, if you have a friend who gets into drugs or alcohol, or engages in other risky behaviors, she may try to get you to participate as well. Although you may want to try to help her, her problems are probably too big for you to handle. Your best bet may be to walk away from the friendship so that you can continue to be a good role model for your other friends.

ATHLETES >> Social media plays a huge factor in everything these days, and athletes have to be smart about how they use it. Kids love to post everything they do, but many don't think about the fact that the college coaches who are investing in them are tracking social media, too.

We had one player who committed to a very well-known, dry university. She had the grades and the talent, and everything looked good to go. One month before she was set to sign her letter of intent, I got a call from the college coach, saying, "Hey, I just wanted to let you know that we are not going to take her."

I was baffled. "Why not? She already committed and everything."

He said, "I know, but she just posted photos on Twitter and Instagram of herself drinking at a party. If she is doing that her senior year, how do you think she is going to be in college? This isn't going to work. If she is partying already, it's going to be a big problem.

She is better off finding a place that suits her than coming here."

Student athletes have got to understand that they are getting a substantial amount of money, in the form of college costs, to play. The majority of scholarships are anywhere between $100,000 and $200,000, over four years. You have to learn to behave and you have to learn how to be smart about how you handle social media.
–Ziad

KASSI MCCLUSKIE >> *As you continue to rise through the levels, you have to be honest about what you are willing to sacrifice for your sport. You will miss birthday parties and dances. I grew up in Arizona, but Thanksgiving, for me, was always spent in California, playing in the Surf Cup Tournament. New Year's Eve was always spent in Florida, playing for another tournament.*

The club I played for growing up in Arizona had very specific rules: our shirts had to be tucked in, we had to maintain discipline while warming up, we had certain ways we had to line up, we always arrived early for practice—all of those little things were part of learning professionalism. Understanding and appreciating sacrifice is part of that. In the real world, you are going to have to sacrifice things to get what you want. It's all about knowing your priorities and your goals.

COMPLETE ATHLETE

JOIN THE CONVERSATION!
Download the Complete Athlete app now!

LIVING YOUR SPORT

Levels 1 and 2 revolved around playing for the love of the game, practicing more, and really studying the rules of soccer. At Level 3, youth players who live the sport of soccer begin really studying professional players, especially those who play the positions they want to play.

HOW TO STUDY PROFESSIONAL PLAYERS »

- Watch professional matches, especially when your favorite players play
- Closely watch the players who play the position(s) you want to play
- Read articles and any books about your favorite players
- Put together a list of questions you'd like to ask if you ever get the opportunity to meet a professional soccer player who plays the position(s) you want to play

COMPLETE ATHLETE

JOIN THE CONVERSATION!
Download the Complete Athlete app now!

MIA HAMM

When I was starting high school, I was a good player and I was fast, but I wasn't great. I enjoyed juggling the ball and working on shots, but I didn't have good endurance and I didn't have a great touch. I remember Anson Dorrance, the national team coach at the time, telling me he was worried about my progress and thought maybe he had brought me up too early with the training program. That was eye-opening for me, because I didn't want to stop playing and I didn't want to give up. What Coach Dorrance was saying to me wasn't "You're not good enough" but "It's more than just being a competitor that's going to keep you on this team. You have to commit to all of it."

I remember going home and asking my dad if I could get a pair of running shoes. I'd never owned a pair just for running, but that was my way of forcing myself to take the training and conditioning seriously, instead of just focusing on certain skills or relying on my sprinting speed. I had always struggled with the fitness side of things, but I realized that I was going to have to make a change to work on endurance if I really wanted to have a chance at success. I also knew that success wasn't going to be the result of my dad standing there with a stopwatch saying, "Do it again!" He could help me and be a part of my training, but the real force behind it had to be me. I had to be the one who wanted it and the one who had the discipline to actually put in the work. Athletes need to be mindful of their personal level of commitment to improving whatever it is that is holding them back, even if it is not the most enjoyable part of playing the game.

Even more important than that, though, is a willingness to put in the discipline to prepare yourself for college.

When I was 14 and just starting to go through the Olympic development program and making the state team, an older player who was just out of college came to work with us, and she and I started talking. She asked me how my grades were and I said, "Oh, they're okay. I'm an okay student." She stopped, looked right at me, and said, "Well, you need to be a great student. Your grades need to be your priority. You should put the same amount of work and commitment into your studies as you do your game."

I remember how much that affected me because I realized that your grades matter for life after soccer. The reality of that situation hit me very hard, and it made a huge impact in terms of how I approached my schoolwork from then on. I realized that I needed to start being more consistent with my investment in studying rather than giving just a little splash of effort the night before a test or the last week of the grading period.

The opportunity to use your talent through the game to get a great education is a gift. Take advantage of that by adding the same discipline you use in soccer to the academic side of your life. You never know when your career is going to end, whether due to an injury or something else. You just never know what is going to happen, but at some point you are going to retire from soccer. At that point, whenever it comes, the value you put on your education is going to pay off. The investment you make there is going to last you a lot longer than your playing career, but the same tools that made you a successful player will translate to a successful academic record: time management, organization, intensity, team-work, and discipline.

IN LEVEL 4

a soccer player must understand what it takes to succeed in college as a student as well as an athlete. As a high-school soccer player, you were 1 of 350,000 in the country. Now you are 1 of only 8,500 of the very best athletes playing at the collegiate level. In order to flourish in college and stand out on the field, you need to make good decisions in every aspect of your life.

4.1 ATTITUDE

A **POSITIVE ATTITUDE** is essential to an athlete's success both on and off the playing field. A positive attitude is something that can be developed with practice, just like any other skill. A **COMPLETE ATHLETE** makes a habit of demonstrating the following five attributes:

RESPECT

SPORTSMANSHIP

TEAMWORK

PROFESSIONALISM

LEADERSHIP

RESPECT

At Level 4, a youth soccer player becomes a college-level student-athlete. By achieving Level 4, a student-athlete has consistently demonstrated **RESPECT** for her coaches, game officials, teammates, and opponents, as well as for herself. These skills will likely be tested while she is in college.

In college, a student-athlete is under a great deal of pressure to perform—both on the field and in the classroom. There are also many more temptations to engage in activities that do not contribute to her health and well-being, such as drinking alcohol or taking performance-enhancing drugs or other illegal substances.

At Level 4, a student-athlete should always demonstrate respect for the game of soccer. Taking performance-enhancing drugs violates the rules as well as the integrity with which she plays, and should be avoided at all times.

ATHLETES » I remember once a player called me from college after a really terrible weekend. Her Friday game didn't go her way, and then her game on Sunday was even worse. When we talked on Monday, my first question to her was, "So, what did you do after your game on Friday?" She didn't really want to answer me, so I asked her again. Finally she admitted that she went out with her friends after the game to a fraternity party, and then she went home and slept in late.

I said, "Okay, can I ask you another question? If that was still Slammers and you had a bad game, what would you have done on Saturday before your game on Sunday?"

"I would have gotten up early and trained," she answered immediately. "I would have taken a bag of balls and gotten my confidence back up and my mind right."

"So what's the difference between Slammers or when you were a club player or when you were a youth player … and now?"

Never forget what got you to where you are now. Never forget your roots. Dealing with a bad game at a collegiate level should be just the same. Going out with your friends or trying to forget the bad game by partying is definitely not the answer. You've got to respect the game and you've got to respect yourself. *–Ziad*

JOIN THE CONVERSATION!
Download the Complete Athlete app now!

COMPLETE
ATHLETE

SPORTSMANSHIP

Good **SPORTSMANSHIP** starts with respect for one's teammates, opponents, coaches, and officials. It also includes maintaining a positive attitude when dealing with adversity—or victory.

At Level 4, the stakes are higher and the pressure to win is greater. Student-athletes often play with a great deal of emotion, putting everything they've got into the game. Some find it difficult to contain their emotions before, during, and at the end of the game.

A Level 4 **COMPLETE ATHLETE** demonstrates good sportsmanship by:

- Not trash-talking the other team or players online or off before the game
- Graciously shaking hands with opponents before and after each game
- Not gloating if her team wins
- Sincerely congratulating the other team if her team loses

ATHLETES » I will never forget when I was watching the NCAA Final Four with one of my teams and at half-time, there was a special reflecting on the best and worst moments of the season. One of the things they highlighted was when a player from one particular school lost control of her emotions during a game, grabbed the other player by her hair, and dragged her down. It was such a violent pull that it almost broke the other girl's neck. It was unbelievable to watch and it was on ESPN. It was one of the most watched clips on YouTube.

When the game was over and we were discussing how it had all played out, I told the girls to reflect back on that moment we saw during half-time. There it was: just one moment of losing control in a game, and it could impact a player for the rest of her career, both on and off the field. Games are streamed live now so anyone can watch them, and there are people who are just waiting for moments like that to capitalize on and make go viral.

I stressed to my players the importance of controlling their emotions, regardless of whether they are winning or losing, regardless of whether someone is trash-talking, regardless of whether someone is playing dirty. Part of being an athlete is dealing with hecklers who just want to get under your skin. They may follow you on Facebook or troll you online, throwing out all sorts of personal information like if you just broke up with your boyfriend or are still with your girlfriend or whatever it is they think they can throw at you to get a rise. There is going to be a situation, sooner or later, where some other player or fan is going to find some way to get under your skin, so you have to be ready to deflect it and use that anger to your advantage, instead of losing focus on the game. It is really, really important that every player be able to shield herself and develop that sense of personal control that is going to make her a **COMPLETE ATHLETE**. –*Ziad*

COACHES » Some of the best days of the year for me as a coach are the weekends from September to December when the NCAA Women's Soccer games are being played. Every Friday and Saturday, I have the opportunity to travel locally or across the country to watch some of my former athletes play. No matter how they perform in the game, my greatest pleasure is just to watch them afterward go right up front to shake hands and congratulate the other team on a good game—win or lose.

I can't tell you what a privilege it is for me to sit there in the bleachers and watch our alumnae demonstrating such sportsmanship, being sincere, controlling their emotions, and being gracious right there at the front of the line. It is a habit we try to ingrain in our players at the youngest levels, and it just makes my heart swell to see them taking those lessons and carrying on that tradition.

I always tell them, "You never know—one day that girl you played against for many years who was always your rival but whom you treated with the utmost respect could be the person across the desk interviewing you for a job." Sportsmanship doesn't just matter on the field; it says so much about your character in real life.

—*Ziad*

COMPLETE ATHLETE

JOIN THE CONVERSATION!
Download the Complete Athlete app now!

TEAMWORK

TEAMWORK means working together as a group in order to achieve a goal. In sports, players contribute their individual skills and efforts in cooperation with their teammates to win games. Learning to play as part of a team, and not just as an individual athlete, is important at every level of play.

By Level 4, a soccer player has dedicated a great deal of her time and energy to get to this point, and she has a right to be proud of her accomplishment. So do her teammates.

At this stage, each member of the team has reached an elite level of play. Soccer is no longer just a game; your team might be playing for a championship at some point. Teammates need to commit to each other to the point of feeling like they are part of a family all working toward a common goal.

It almost feels like an earlier level at which the members of the team needed to learn to trust each other in order to work together as an effective team. Team-building exercises should be taken very seriously, and any personality issues must be worked out immediately.

ATHLETES >> Something that trips up a lot of players when they move into the collegiate level is that, for the first time in their soccer career, it's not a year-round club. Because of the NCAA rules, there are four or five months when the coaches cannot be involved with you or have any official practices. That's where the teamwork has to come in.

It is especially important for incoming freshmen that they don't waste that four-month gap. Use it to train independent of the coach—but work as if the coach were watching! In the top programs, like Florida State and North Carolina, you see the whole team working out together in the morning. They do pick-up games at night, finding indoor arenas to play five-on-five. This is the only way that these players are going to stay sharp, compete at the highest levels, and be able to contribute to their team's success. —*Walid*

PROFESSIONALISM

As a youth soccer player becomes a student-athlete, **PROFESSIONALISM** takes on a new meaning. She now plays for a college team, and she needs to represent that team with dignity and pride—both on and off the field, as well as on- and offline. Not doing so can have serious consequences in terms of any scholarships she may have received.

A student-athlete should always maintain professionalism in terms of her appearance, her attitude, and her actions. Some examples include:

- Learning rules of etiquette and always displaying good manners
- Dressing appropriately off the field—no obscene T-shirts, no skimpy clothing, etc.
- Wearing team apparel that represents her college or university, not another one
- Keeping her online presence uncontroversial
- Staying away from inappropriate situations, such as parties where drugs may be present
- Avoiding the bar scene, especially if she is underage

COMPLETE ATHLETE

JOIN THE CONVERSATION!
Download the Complete Athlete app now!

LEADERSHIP

A youth soccer player may have become a team **LEADER** in high school. As she moves on to college play, she may hope to continue in that role. A leader for a college-level team must be able to:

- Communicate effectively and present expectations clearly
- Listen patiently and open-mindedly to the input and opinions of others
- Treat all teammates fairly and never play favorites
- Be open and honest with teammates

ATHLETES » In the off-season, as a leader for your team at a collegiate level, you have responsibilities both on and off the field. Since NCAA rules do not allow teams to train year-round, you need to step up and provide that guidance during the times your season is not actively underway. Your team needs to stay in practice, which is why a good leader needs to have the right attitude for keeping things on track.

Most teams have a number of awards—MVP, best defensive player, best offensive player—but especially at the collegiate level, leadership is so essential to the success of the team that every single program I know of has an award to honor the player that best espouses those traits. For coaches, one of the hardest things is to identify these natural leaders on each team and then to feel comfortable essentially giving them the keys to the car during the off-season.

On the field, you are functioning in some ways as a coach, because you are helping to drive practice in lieu of your official coach—steering your teammates from one drill to the next, dictating when breaks start and end, holding your teammates accountable for their effort and what they are putting into the practice. Even though there are no specific games to plan for, you still have to be able to motivate your teammates to stay engaged in keeping up with their skills, training, fitness, and eligibility.

As a team leader off the field, you are following up with all the players on how they are doing in their classes, and reminding them to make good choices about how and when they socialize. If you lead by example and show your teammates you are more concerned about serving the good of the team rather than your own individual glory, they will be far more willing to follow you.

Camille Levin is a fantastic example of someone who understood the importance of this kind of servant leadership. She was a leader on her team during the off-season and proved her commitment to team over self by the way she played. In the National Championship game against Duke, she went down the line from the outside back, dribbled past several players, and lost the ball, but she didn't give up on it. There was a slight tackle, but she got the ball back and crossed it to a teammate—who actually scored the goal. Even though she was the one who really drove that ball the length of the field and could have reasoned that the shot was really "hers" to take, she instead passed it to a teammate who was in a better position to score. She had always led from a place of toughness but selflessness. And that toughness and selflessness made all the difference. Her team was seasoned and ready to block their opponents in a gruelingly physical game, and the pass she made, rather than take the shot herself, resulted in the point that won the game and the title. –*Walid and Ziad*

CAMILLE LEVIN >> *My freshman year at Stanford, I was two weeks into pre-season when the coaches suddenly said, "We're going to put you at center-mid because we think you can do it." I had been recruited as a right wing and that was what I played in the national team system, too, so that was a bit of a shake-up for me. But I was also pretty excited at the chance, because there were two upperclassmen who also played right wing and obviously wanted a spot on the field, so I would have ended up behind them. Changing positions meant that I would have more time on the field, so I was willing to do it in order to play. I ended up playing center-mid the entire season, and it was a great year! We made it to the final four and lost just one game that season.*

My senior year of college, I played as a winger most of the season. But right before the national title tournament, our center-back went down and our coach tapped me to move to her position, even though I had never played it before. I knew that it was the best thing for our team, though, so I went with it.

You have to stay confident and know that you are being put there for a reason. I reminded myself that this was the tournament—not a time to gamble. The coach would not be putting me in that position unless he was confident with that decision. I knew my team and I was confident in them. Sure, your mentality changes a little bit based on your position, because you have different roles; but at the end of the day, it is still the same game you've played for so long.

4.2 PREPARATION

At the college level, **PREPARATION** takes on a whole new importance. It is more than just your personal discipline with practice, diet, rest, and mentality; it also involves watching game tapes, studying your opponents, and being emotionally focused both on and off the field. Athletes who prepare for every game and practice naturally emerge as team leaders. These are the players who make the starting roster because they have a winning attitude that drives the way they hone their skills and prioritize their time and academics.

A **COMPLETE ATHLETE** prepares to perform on the field of play by continuously improving on the following:

PRACTICE

NUTRITION

HYDRATION

RECOVERY

MENTALITY

PRACTICE

At Level 4, an athlete is playing soccer at the college level, and **PRACTICE** sessions are supervised by an elite coaching staff. However, because they are working with an entire team of soccer players, that staff will be limited in the time they are able to spend with each individual athlete. In addition, at NCAA colleges and universities, rules are in place to limit the amount of practice and conditioning time required by and supervised by the coaches.

Student-athletes who want to achieve higher levels of success—or even just want to maintain the success they've already achieved—must practice drills and perform con-ditioning activities independently or alongside team-mates without the direct supervision of the coaches.

HOW TO WORK INDEPENDENTLY OF COACHES ≫

- Develop your own practice schedules that include the skills you want or need to improve as well as those you've already mastered.
- Create a conditioning schedule that allows you to work each muscle group with at least one day of rest in between.
- Incorporate the technical knowledge you've gained up to this point.
- Listen to your body to train and practice safely with minimal risk of injury.
- Continue to practice and perform conditioning activities throughout the off-season to maintain your athleticism.
- If possible, continue to work with a private coach.

ATHLETES >> Of all the resources available at the college level, access to game tapes is one of the most valuable. Often, players will call us and say, "I had a bad game and I don't know what I did wrong."

The first thing we suggest is checking out the recording of the game. A lot of schools now even offer individual DVDs for each player, where they break it down so that each athlete can see every time she touched the ball. Players have to take advantage of that, because the video doesn't lie—it will show you what you did right and what you did wrong.

If you take that seriously and really study what happened as you watch, you can think about your weaknesses more objectively and arrive at practice early the next day to work on whatever you need to, or stay late and work with the assistant coach on the specific issue you're having. That makes your practice more effective.

Camille Levin could dribble through everybody, but her one weakness was crossing. She started to study herself on tape as a scholarship player at Stanford, and then she began drilling to improve. In the national championship game against Duke, she dribbled through everybody and then came to the byline and hit the one cross that went past everyone and onto the head of a teammate to fire into the goal and win the title. If she had not taken advantage of those videos in order to study her weaknesses, that moment probably never would have occurred. *—Walid and Ziad*

NUTRITION

As a youth soccer player becomes a college student-athlete, **NUTRITION** continues to play a key role in her life, not only for optimal performance on the field of play, but also to obtain the vitamins and minerals she needs for optimal health.

LEVEL 4 ATHLETE NUTRITION GUIDELINES »

Each individual has different macronutrient needs, based on height, weight, age, activity level, and genetic background. The following macronutrient guidelines are based on age and estimated activity level for a Level-4 athlete:

- 45% carbohydrate
- 30% protein
- 25% fat
- No more than 7% saturated fat
- No trans fat
- 38 grams of fiber per day
- No more than 150 calories per day from sugar (37.5 grams or 9 teaspoons)

ATHLETES » One of the best things about playing at a university is that you have full-time nutritionists there to work with the teams and individual athletes. We tell our players one of the first things to do when you arrive at college is to get to know that nutritionist—learn his or her name, remember it, and establish a good relationship. That person is going to play a huge part in your collegiate career if you take advantage of having that resource at your disposal. Check in with the nutritionist, listen to what he or she is telling you, and eat and drink what they advise you to; they are professionals and have mastered what an athlete really needs for fuel as well as for recovery. Your nutritionist's advice can be the thing that gives you the edge over other players, so make sure you follow it! *–Walid and Ziad*

HYDRATION

Athletes should drink water before, during, and after practices and games. This is especially important on days when both temperatures and humidity levels are high.

HOW TO MAINTAIN PROPER HYDRATION*>>

- Before exercise, drink 16–20 full ounces within the 2-hour period prior to exercise.
- During exercise, drink 4–6 full ounces.
- After exercise, replace 24 full ounces for every one pound of body weight lost during exercise.
- * *Adapted from guidelines provided by the American College of Sports Medicine (ACSM)*

ATHLETES >> At the collegiate level, you are practicing more than you've ever practiced. You're training five times a week, plus games—and the intensity and the speed of play increases. You are up against players who are older, stronger, and more experienced than you. Hydration plays a large part in how you're going to perform at this level, so make sure you are constantly hydrating. Take advantage of the Gatorade on the sidelines; carry a water bottle with you at all times. Make sure you are getting fluids in your system, because it's going to be a huge X-factor in your performance.

RECOVERY

Youth athletes need to eat and drink within 30 minutes of a practice or game to make up for the calories they are burning and fluids they are using. Replenishing calories and fluids also aids in muscle **RECOVERY** and repair.

HOW TO REPLENISH CALORIES AND FLUIDS »

- Drink 24 ounces of fluid for every pound of sweat lost within a 2-hour period of a game or practice.
- Consume 25–30 grams of protein plus an equal amount of carbohydrates within the 30-minute recovery window.

SLEEP Getting adequate sleep is difficult during this stage. Typically college student athletes are "burning the candle on both ends"; in other words, they're up early in the morning and also up late in the evening.

According to the National Sleep Foundation, a Level-4 student-athlete should get 7–9 hours of sleep each night. If you sleep six hours or less on a consistent basis, you may be setting yourself up for failure, because your body cannot perform at an optimal level. Sleep deprivation can also affect hormone regulation, which makes your body crave more sugar and refined carbohydrates for quick energy. That is the opposite of what your body needs.

COMPLETE
ATHLETE

JOIN THE CONVERSATION!
Download the Complete Athlete app now!

TIPS FOR GETTING MORE SLEEP IN COLLEGE* >>

AVOID STIMULANTS, such as coffee and energy drinks. If you must drink them, do so earlier in the day, and cut yourself off by noon.

WIND DOWN. Your body needs time to shift into sleep mode, so spend the last hour before bed doing a calming activity, such as reading. Avoid using an electronic device, such as a laptop, because the particular type of light emanating from the screens of these devices is activating to the brain.

PRACTICE A RELAXING BEDTIME RITUAL. A relaxing, routine activity right before bedtime, conducted away from bright lights, helps separate your sleep time from activities that can cause excitement, stress, or anxiety and that can make it more difficult to fall asleep, get sound and deep sleep, or remain asleep.

* *Adapted from the National Sleep Foundation*

ATHLETES >> The college season is condensed into a three-month period, which is so different from youth-level sports, which tend to go most of the year. As a result, the recovery period is greatly reduced, too.

One former player of ours admitted that her secret to doing so well in college play was ear plugs. "When you have roommates and parties in the dorms and you need to get to bed early," she said, "just stick in some ear plugs or headphones with a little music, and go to sleep."

On the other hand, some players try to find a balance between academics and sports by relying on Red Bull and coffee to keep them awake—but that means that

they have so much caffeine pumping through their veins that they can't sleep when they try. It is very important to find the balance so that you can allow your body the rest and recovery it needs to keep you in peak shape.
–*Walid and Ziad*

MENTALITY

Being a better athlete does not necessarily mean training harder or longer. Certainly a youth soccer player must spend time physically preparing her body to meet the demands of a practice session or game. Similarly, engaging in **MENTAL PREPARATION** can help her perform at a higher level by creating the proper mindset for either practice or a game.

At Level 4, the focus is on learning mental imagery. Mental imagery is simply seeing yourself perform successfully before you even step on the field of play. Student-athletes who can envision themselves performing successfully will perform better.

Mental imagery takes practice and requires a great deal of concentration. However, the more you train your mind to focus on the right things, the more it will respond. Using all of your senses helps. For example, imagine the smell of the grass as you move along the field of play. See yourself getting ready to perform a penalty kick. Feel your foot as it moves to kick the ball, and hear the sound it makes as it connects with the ball. Finally, envision a perfect penalty kick.

ATHLETES >> Again, at the collegiate level, athletes should take advantage of the resources schools have in place to help their scholarship athletes excel. Work with the sports psychologist on staff, or try some kind of yoga or meditation—whatever is available to you, give it a try. There is a reason those different options and opportunities are there, so don't be afraid to explore outside the box.

KASSI MCCLUSKIE >> *I was an emotional player. I'm not ashamed to admit that I sometimes cried when we lost because I wanted to be the better team. I think many of us are like that, and I think it is something we should embrace.*

Sometimes, female athletes feel like they have to "toughen up" and not allow themselves to show any emotion because emotion is often seen as a sign of weakness. Some women really are naturally unemotional or understated with their feelings; if that is the way you are, that's great. But if you are like me and you really wear your heart on your sleeve when you play, don't think you have to change who you are or hide how you feel—that can sometimes make you even more emotional because you end up feeling like you have to bottle everything up. Instead, I suggest you channel all those feelings into your game.

I wish, when I was younger, that someone had told me to embrace my emotion and make it part of my playing style. It would have helped me recognize my unique playing style and approach to leadership much sooner. It's okay to let people know you care about your game! If that's who you are, pour your heart into your game and don't think you ever need to be ashamed or embarrassed of that aspect of yourself.

COMPLETE ATHLETE

JOIN THE CONVERSATION!
Download the Complete Athlete app now!

4.3 FITNESS

At Level 4, a soccer player is at the college level. She likely has a strength-and-conditioning coach who super-vises fitness workouts. However, because that coach is working with an entire team of soccer players, he or she will be limited in the time spent with each individual athlete. In addition, at NCAA colleges and uni-versities, rules are in place to limit the amount of practice and conditioning time required by and supervised by the coaches.

Student-athletes who want to achieve higher levels of **FITNESS**—or even just want to maintain the level of fitness they've already achieved—must perform conditioning activities independently or alongside teammates with-out the direct supervision of the coaches. Not only does this help to establish a foundation of good fitness, but it also teaches good habits needed for success in higher levels of soccer.

LOWER-BODY STRENGTH

UPPER-BODY STRENGTH

FLEXIBILITY / MOBILITY

CORE STRENGTH

SPEED / QUICKNESS / ENDURANCE

LOWER-BODY STRENGTH

Level 4 builds on what you have done in Level 3. You should be getting stronger, more explosive, and better balanced. You will see that strength in the lower body has been the difference in keeping you healthy and dynamic on the pitch. At this level, you may be trying to make a college starting roster or even a national team roster. Chances are, your skills are at a very high level; now, you must have elite-level strength in your lower body to set yourself apart from the rest. We are pushing your test numbers higher because we know you are nearing the top of the food chain in soccer, which very few athletes reach; separators are usually in the work ethic and strength. Your times are extended, the reps are higher, and the distances have increased.

TO PERFORM SINGLE-LEG WALL SQUATS >>

- Stand on one leg while your other leg is lifted off the ground in front of the body. Your hip should be bent to approximately 45 degrees and your knee bent to approximately 90 degrees.
- Hold your arms out straight in front of you with your hands clasped together. From this position, squat down until your knee is bent to approximately 60 degrees.
- Return to the start position and repeat.

COMPLETE ATHLETE

JOIN THE CONVERSATION!
Download the Complete Athlete app now!

TO PERFORM A SINGLE-LEG WALL SIT »

- Stand with your back against a smooth vertical wall and your feet approximately shoulder-width apart.
- Slowly slide your back down the wall until both knees and hips are at a 90-degree angle.
- Lift one foot off the ground and hold it as long as possible. After a period of rest, lift the other foot and hold it.

NOTE » If you can hold one foot up considerably longer than the other, you may need to work on developing a better balance of strength in both legs.

TO PERFORM A BROAD JUMP »

- Stand behind a line marked on the ground, with your feet slightly apart.
- Use a two-foot takeoff and landing, swinging your arms and bending your knees to provide drive.
- Jump as far as possible, landing on both feet without falling backward.

NOTE » The broad jump is a great linear measurement of power in the legs.

TO PERFORM A VERTICAL JUMP TEST »

- Stand next to any wall and, with your feet completely flat, reach up with your hand closest to the wall and measure the highest point you can touch. (This is easier to do with two people so the other person can mark and measure.)
- With your arm still raised, jump as high as you can and note how high you are able to touch.

- Measure the distance between the two points for your vertical jump score.

UPPER-BODY STRENGTH

College coaches are looking to separate the best players from the competition, so the margin for error is small. Your **UPPER-BODY STRENGTH** may be the difference between getting up slowly or quickly to re-engage your opponent after a fall.

As expressed in previous levels, you need to keep up your upper-body conditioning to play at higher levels of soccer.

Pull exercises are used to increase upper-back strength and mobility, while push exercises increase chest and shoulder strength and mobility.

TO PERFORM A VERTICAL PULL-UP >>

- Grasp an overhead bar using the neutral grip or underhand grip (palms facing toward body), with your arms fully extended and your legs hanging straight down.
- Raise your body up until your chin clears the top of the bar.
- Lower again to the starting position, with your arms fully extended.

TO PERFORM PUSH-UPS »

- Lie face down on the floor (or mat) with your hands under your shoulders or slightly wider than your chest, fingers straight, legs straight and parallel.
- Straighten your arms, pushing your upper body up and keeping your back and knees straight.
- Bend your arms to lower your upper body until your elbows are at a 90-degree angle and your upper arms are parallel to the floor.
- Perform as many repetitions as possible without resting.

TO PERFORM AN OVERHEAD MEDICINE-BALL THROW »

- Stand with both feet on a line, facing forward.
- Hold a medicine ball with both hands and raise it above and behind your head.
- Draw the ball back and throw it as far as possible in front of you at a 45-degree angle.
- It is okay to follow through past the line after throwing.

COMPLETE
ATHLETE

JOIN THE CONVERSATION!
Download the Complete Athlete
app now!

FLEXIBILITY / MOBILITY

A good degree of **FLEXIBILITY** and **MOBILITY** leads to better soccer technique and helps to prevent injuries. As discussed in previous levels, the sit-and-reach test is used to assess—and improve—a youth athlete's level of lower-body flexibility and mobility.

TO PERFORM THE SIT-AND-REACH TEST >>

NOTE >> You'll need a box that is 12 inches high, such as a milk crate. Tape a yardstick or ruler to the top so that the first nine inches hang over the edge and the nine-inch mark is exactly on the edge against which you will place your feet.

- Place the box against a wall.
- Sit on the floor in front of the box with your legs straight in front of you and the soles of your feet flat against the front side of the box. The overhanging part of the ruler should be pointed at your chest or midsection.
- Keeping your legs straight and flat on the floor, stretch forward and reach along the ruler with one hand on top of the other, palms down.
- Stretch forward three times without bouncing; then reach as far as possible, holding the farthest point for at least three seconds.

The purpose of the 90/90 test is to determine if the athlete has tight hamstrings and is at risk of possible leg injury. A failure in this test means you need to stretch more to gain more flexibility.

TO PERFORM A 90/90 TEST >>

- Lie on your back, legs straight and flat on the ground.
- Bend the test knee to 90 degrees and then raise it so your thigh is vertical and your knee still bent. (The non-test leg should still be straight and resting on the floor.)
- Bend at the knee to straighten your test leg. If you can extend your leg to 0 degrees (the entire leg is straight at a 90-degree angle from your body), you have passed. If you cannot straighten your leg, record what angle you have left to achieve neutral position (straight knee). Anything greater than 10 degrees is failing. (Make sure the non-test leg never bends or comes off the ground while measuring.)

CORE STRENGTH

Now that you are in an exclusive group of athletic achievement, the slightest differentiations can give you a major edge. An athlete who has better balance and stability will have the advantage over one who doesn't, and this is exactly what a strong core gives you. We are keeping the plank, medicine-ball throw, hip-lift march, and side plank to your test.

The plank and the side plank are great exercises for strengthening your core.

TO PERFORM A PLANK >>

- Get down on the floor with your hands slightly wider than shoulder-width apart and your arms straight and supporting your weight.
- Make sure your body stays straight—your hips shouldn't be sticking way up in the air or sagging.
- Hold this position for as long as you can.

COMPLETE ATHLETE

JOIN THE CONVERSATION!
Download the Complete Athlete app now!

TO PERFORM A SIDE PLANK »

- Lie on your side with your legs straight.
- Prop your upper body up on your elbow and forearm. Make sure your elbow is aligned with your shoulder.
- Brace your core by contracting your abs forcefully and then raise your hips until your body forms a straight line from your ankles to your shoulders.
- Breathe deeply while holding this position.
- Repeat this exercise on your other side.

The hip-lift march helps to measure—and improve—the strength and endurance of your back muscles.

TO PERFORM A HIP-LIFT MARCH »

- Lie flat on your back with your knees bent 90 degrees and your feet flat on the ground.
- Lift your hips as high as possible, with only your shoulders and feet touching the ground.
- While keeping your hips at the same height, lift each knee in a controlled marching motion for as long as possible.

SPEED / QUICKNESS / ENDURANCE

There are two types of soccer speed:

- Straightaway speed on an open field
- Lateral (side-to-side) quickness

The 30-yard sprint helps an athlete improve straight-away speed. The 5-10-5 shuttle run, or pro agility drill, improves lateral quickness, because it helps to hone an athlete's ability to accelerate, decelerate, stop, and reaccelerate without losing balance. The beep test is a good way to measure and improve endurance.

TO PERFORM A 30-YARD SPRINT »

- Place two cones 30 yards apart.
- Starting at one cone, run as fast as you can to the other cone.

TO PERFORM A 5-10-5 SHUTTLE RUN »

- Set up three marker cones five yards apart.
- Start at the middle marker cone in a three-point stance.
- Turn and run five yards to the right side and touch the marker cone with your right hand.
- Turn around and run 10 yards to the left and touch the marker cone with your left hand.
- Turn and finish by running back to the middle marker cone.

NOTE » Always run forward while altering your running direction, as opposed to strictly stopping and starting in opposite directions. Be sure to alternate sides each time—first time curve to the left, second time curve to the right.

TO PERFORM A BEEP TEST »

NOTE » You'll first need to download a beep test audio recording or beep test app, which will play beeps at set intervals. As the test proceeds, the interval between successive beeps reduces, forcing the athlete to increase her speed.

- Draw two lines 40 yards apart.
- Stand behind one of the lines, facing the second line, and begin running when instructed by the recording.
- Continue running between the two lines, turning when signaled by the recorded beeps. After about one minute, a sound indicates an increase in speed, and the beeps will become closer together.
- The test is stopped when the athlete can no longer keep in sync with the recording.

COMPLETE ATHLETE

JOIN THE CONVERSATION!
Download the Complete Athlete app now!

LEVEL-4 FITNESS TEST

LOWER-BODY STRENGTH »

- 10 full-range single-leg squats on each leg
- Single-leg wall squat for at least 75 seconds
- Broad jump of 86 inches or more
- Vertical jump of 19 inches or more

UPPER-BODY STRENGTH »

- Bent-arm hold pull-up for 30 seconds
- 40 push-ups in 60 seconds

FLEXIBILITY/MOBILITY »

- Sit-and-reach test score of at least 40 centimeters
- 90/90 test is pass or fail

CORE STRENGTH/BALANCE »

- Plank for 2 $\frac{1}{2}$ minutes
- Side plank for 50 seconds on each side
- Hip-lift march with perfect form for 2 $\frac{1}{2}$ minutes
- Single-leg balance on each leg for 45 seconds
- Standing overhead 6-pound medicine-ball throw of at least 7 $\frac{1}{2}$ yards

SPEED/QUICKNESS/ENDURANCE »

- 5-10-5 shuttle run in 5 seconds
- 30-yard sprint in 4.6 seconds
- Beep test minimum score of 7/2-8/5 (number of levels/number of shuttles completed)

4.4 TECHNIQUE

Level 4 is a very high level of soccer requiring the importance of shifts to the ability to perform in pressured situations during games. Remember that a **COMPLETE ATHLETE** not only masters the basic and advanced skills needed to play the game of soccer, but she also understands the roles and responsibilities of every position on a team and how all the positions work together to win games. Moving into the collegiate level, all the skills that you learned in Levels 1, 2, and 3 need to be used at an even higher level of efficiency, speed, and thinking in order to perform in big-game environments. These skills include:

FOUNDATIONAL BALL SKILLS / DRIBBLING

PASSING

BALL CONTROL

BALL-STRIKING / SHOOTING

HEADING

FOUNDATIONAL BALL SKILLS / DRIBBLING

- Improving your moves to 7-8, with emphasis on using both feet to execute
- Using your speed/pace with the ball at the right moments, because most opponents will have similar athletic abilities
- Being aggressive in the right areas to read the covering defender
- Deception with upper and lower body to put opponent off-balance
- Ability to use creative skill to pick the best side to get in behind opponents

PASSING

- Ability to weight the ball in to feet or lead them
- Driving balls with ranges of 40 to 50 yards
- Bending the ball to switch the field or cross in the final third
- Chipping the ball with the right weight and timing with teammate
- Using the outside of the foot for deception and to release a quick outlet
- Heel and flick passing to find creative movement off of opponents

COMPLETE ATHLETE

JOIN THE CONVERSATION!
Download the Complete Athlete app now!

BALL CONTROL

- Using all surfaces of the feet and body
- Receiving the ball with the inside or outside of both feet to create space
- Ability to turn with both feet inside or outside to penetrate
- Controlling the ball 40 to 50 yards with both feet
- Turning with the ball out of the air or on the bounce

BALL-STRIKING / SHOOTING

- Finishing with the instep to drive inside and outside of the box
- Inside-of-the-foot finishing
- Bending the ball to finish in the right areas
- Chipping the ball to finish when the goalkeeper is out of position
- Inside-of-the-foot volleys from wide service
- Outside-of-the-foot to catch the goalkeeper off guard
- Volley or full on the side when the ball arrives to your body in the right way to connect

HEADING

- For distance, technical power
- Flicking on or heading down to find teammate
- Clearing wide
- Timing to arrive in the box to flick down or snap across to score

4.5 LIFESTYLE

A Level-4 soccer player has achieved a great feat: playing at the college level. Chances are, she has earned an athletic scholarship, an academic scholarship, or both. As a college-level student athlete, she will need to employ all of the time-management and organization skills learned throughout this journey in order to maintain a satisfactory balance between the following elements:

FAMILY

ACADEMICS

SOCIAL LIFE AND ROLE MODEL

LIVING YOUR SPORT

FAMILY

A soccer player who has achieved Level 4 **COMPLETE ATHLETE** status has already laid the foundation for a lifelong positive relationship with her **FAMILY**. While at college, she should strive to maintain those positive relationships by:

KEEPING IN TOUCH Set aside a specific day and time each week to talk to your family by phone. You can also communicate regularly via e-mail or text messaging.

STAYING IN THE LOOP Even though you're living elsewhere, you'll want to feel connected with your family. Make sure your family keeps you informed and included in important family decisions, activities, and updates.

VISITING FACE TO FACE Discuss with your family options for spending time together face-to-face during holidays, birthdays, or other special events. Be actively involved in the planning so that you can work around important sports and/or academic responsibilities.

PARENTS AND COACHES » The freshman year of college is almost always the hardest one in terms of transitioning. It is certainly when I get the most phone calls from my alumnae who are upset and needing support and reassurance. Family members and coaches have to be there for those players and really take the time to listen to them and let them know that what they're going through is normal.

The pressure will come, either from the faster pace of the games, or from a player thinking she's going to be the superstar just coming into the program, or from a player expecting a great deal of playing time but getting bumped out by another player. She ends up depressed and wondering what happened and how.

When my former players call me and they are in this emotional rut, I say, "You know what? All you can do is just work hard and keep on working. Don't make any excuses. The moment will come when a coach is going to tell you to get in the game. You've got to be ready for that moment. If you deliver, you're going to stay on the field. If you're not ready for that moment, prepared for that moment mentally, you're going to fail. You have to get ready and stay ready." And the way she prepares for that moment is for the parents and former coaches to be willing to walk her through that difficult adjustment period of new roommates and responsibilities, difficult classes, and being away from home, friends, family, former teammates, and everything familiar. When these young women reach out to their parents and coaches, they need to know they have a support system that wants the best for them.

One former player of mine was an absolute star and got a scholarship to UCLA—but then one day I got a call from her saying, "I can't do it. I can't do it. Can you come and get me?" So my daughter and I drove to UCLA together, since they had played high school soccer together, and when we arrived at her dorm, this player was already waiting at the curb with all of her bags packed. She threw all of her stuff in the trunk of the car, climbed in the back, and said, "Please, please, just take off." She seemed like she was having an anxiety attack so I just told her to relax, and I took my time listening to her. I asked what was going on and let her express her feelings. They key is not to cut them off but to allow them to be as open and honest as possible. They want to be heard when they reach out to parents and coaches—don't brush them off.

I drove this player home, and she wanted me to tell her parents that she was going to transfer out of UCLA and into a small private school. I told her not to make any rash decisions but just to talk to her parents, so she did. Her parents said no, they did not want her to transfer, but they did want her to be happy. We just took our time working it out. I kind of played the facilitator between the player and her parents, helping her give voice to her feelings but also helping to provide a measured perspective. In the end, she decided to stay at UCLA.

Those are common stories. The transitions can be so difficult, but are so important. If we don't listen to those kids when they want to tell us about their challenges and problems on and off the field, they might go down avenues or make choices that will ultimately hurt their lives and their careers. *–Ziad*

JOIN THE CONVERSATION!
Download the Complete Athlete app now!

COMPLETE
ATHLETE

ACADEMICS

Many student-athletes assume they'll go on to play their sport professionally after college, or even before graduating. The truth is, there are more than 460,000 NCAA student-athletes, and fewer than two percent will go pro in their sports.

The experiences of college athletics and the life lessons student-athletes learn along the way will help them as they pursue a career in any field. Student-athletes should take advantage of every resource and opportunity available to them at the college or university they attend. In fact, many NCAA colleges and universities provide special resources to their student-athletes, including:

ACADEMIC TUTORS for both group and individualized tutoring

ACADEMIC CENTERS that include tutoring space, individual and group study spaces, computer labs, and more

INDIVIDUALIZED ACADEMIC COUNSELING to help student-athletes develop a plan for successfully managing their academic pursuits and reaching their academic goals

CAREER DEVELOPMENT RESOURCES, including career-placement services for summer internships and job opportunities, résumé workshops, alumni networking, e-mail updates for job fairs and internship postings, and more

Whether or not a student-athlete intends to go on to pursue soccer at the professional level, she should absolutely maintain her grades throughout college and graduate with a degree in a marketable field. After all, even a professional sports career will not last forever, and a college graduate will have more opportunities available than one who has not earned a degree.

ATHLETES » In college, the balance of time is so critical because a typical women's soccer schedule from August to December goes something like this: morning practice from 5:30 to 7:00; classes until 2:00; afternoon practice; homework; sleep. That's not even taking into account traveling and road games. You absolutely have to take advantage of the resources that are given to you by the university to help keep your academics in line. There is a reason these resources exist, and it is because the school knows the amount of time student-athletes have available is not like most other students'.

You need to remember that you are a student-athlete, not an athlete-student or an athlete-athlete. If you want to keep your grades up and stay eligible, you have to be willing to use the resources made available by the university. And parents should keep an eye on what classes their child is taking, because students sometimes want to take easy classes just so they can get the grades. Athletes, remember that you are getting a scholarship for this, so maximize what you're getting the scholarship for and take the classes that are going to help you in your career post-college and outside the sports world. –*Walid and Ziad*

COMPLETE
ATHLETE

JOIN THE CONVERSATION!
Download the Complete Athlete app now!

SOCIAL LIFE AND ROLE MODEL

At Level 3, soccer players learned how to recognize and value a true friend and be a good role model to others. These attributes are also important at Level 4. With all the pressures on student-athletes, having strong friendships is vital to their emotional health. True friends will listen and sympathize when that's needed, and they will provide fun and companionship when that's needed. Once again, it's important to be considerate of friends' time and other commitments, and to be responsible when it comes to one's own commitments. Nonetheless, carving out time for friends is an important part of a balanced lifestyle.

When it comes to socializing at college, the temptations to behave badly are many, and the consequences can be dire. There are parties at which alcohol may be served. Illegal drugs and other substances are often readily available on college campuses. Stressed-out friends may engage in impulsive, dangerous behavior and insist that you join them.

Student-athletes can be kicked off the team and lose their scholarships for many reasons. Their best bet is to continue to be a good role model by avoiding social situations that can get them into trouble.

ATHLETE >> It's very important, when you first get to college as an incoming freshman, to start watching the older players. Pick out one or two who represent to you who you want to be when you are an upperclassman.

This is an important exercise for staying on track, because too many athletes come to college focused but slip into partying by the second semester. If you carefully study the players you most want to be like, you'll notice that they tend to be the ones who are the earliest to practice, who put in extra work when needed, who do very well academically, and who stay on top of their homework and tests. Follow their examples not just during the season, but during the off-season, too. Allow them to lead by example.

LIVING YOUR SPORT

At Level 3, players who live the sport of soccer begin studying professional players, especially those that play the positions they want to play. This activity will continue at Level 4, as the student-athlete becomes even more of a student of the game and an enthusiastic fan.

One professional recruiter told the story of a student-athlete who, when asked about her favorite player, talked about a lesser-known player in glowing terms. The recruiter immediately recognized someone who was a true student of the game.

COMPLETE ATHLETE

JOIN THE CONVERSATION!
Download the Complete Athlete app now!

MIA HAMM

Confidence and self-reliance are absolutely essential for succeeding in college.

One thing I have learned after working as a coach is that the older you get, the less people are going to work to bring you in if they see you aren't committed. When you're younger, people will work really hard to draw you in and say, "Come on! Let's be part of the group now." And if you say, "No, no, no, I don't want to," and run away, an adult will run after you and bring you back. The older a child gets, the less energy people are willing to spend trying to engage them to be a part of things. It is also true in the classroom and in the professional world. If you are applying for a job and the first thing you say is, "I'm not really sure I want to work here ... ," the interview is over. If you show up for class and you're not prepared or organized, the professor has 100 other students to worry about; he or she is not going to bend over backward to accommodate you or chase you down for missing assignments. You have to be willing and able to show up and be all in—and that can be tough if you've always relied on your parents to take care of everything.

Literally the day after I graduated from high school, my family moved overseas for six years because my dad was in the military. I had arrangements to stay with a friend over the summer until it was time to leave for school, so I was really in a sink-or-swim situation; I couldn't just drive home for the weekend if something didn't work out the way I wanted it to. I had to figure out how to make things work. That is one of the most important ways of thinking for successful college athletes. You have to be all in and you have to be determined to make it all work out.

I went to the University of North Carolina at Chapel Hill, and athletes didn't get any perks when it came to scheduling, no matter what time our practices were. You just had to figure out how to make things work. When I was enrolled, drop/adds were all handled by hand instead of by computer. Tables were set up for each class in the gym during registration, and people would bring by index cards with the classes they were changing and you just had to wait and hope that someone dropped off a card with the class and time you needed. I remember lying on the floor all day long, just waiting for the 9:00-AM political science class I needed to open up. If someone came by with a card, I would pop up and ask if it was the 9:00 class. If they said it was the 11:00, I just had to say, "Okay, thanks," lie back down, and wait for the next person to come along. I got the class eventually, but it literally took hours of patience, waiting, and asking. You have to be willing to be proactive and take responsibility for getting done what needs doing, no matter how unpleasant or inconvenient.

It is also very important to find mentors in your program to help you learn the ropes and stay on course. Carla Overbeck was a senior when I was a freshman, and we ended up playing on the national team together. In college, though, it was great being able to study how she handled herself and managed to play and succeed in her classes and just navigate everything. Just having someone who has been through it and understands things a bit more fully can instill such a sense of confidence during that first year or two, when everything is so new and can be so overwhelming. That is such an important tool for success: be willing to be mentored— and then take someone under your wing once you're one of the veteran players.

IN LEVEL 5

a soccer player has reached the highest level of her career. She is now a professional athlete. You have made it to the top; now how do you stay there? Maintaining good fitness and nutrition habits will help extend your playing years, but truly great players aren't just stars in the game. They are representatives of their teams, their families, and their beliefs. Learn how to be a good role model as you express yourself on social media, in public, and in the press, and as you interact with fans.

5.1 ATTITUDE

A positive **ATTITUDE** is essential to any athlete's success both on and off the playing field. A Level-5 **COMPLETE ATHLETE** makes a habit of demonstrating the following five attributes:

RESPECT

SPORTSMANSHIP

TEAMWORK

PROFESSIONALISM

LEADERSHIP

RESPECT

As a Level-5 **COMPLETE ATHLETE**, you must continue to demonstrate respect for your coaches and game officials, your teammates, and your opponents, as well as yourself. As a professional soccer player, you should also demonstrate **RESPECT** for the fans who come to see you and your team play. If someone asks for your autograph, be gracious and friendly. Remember, without the fans, you might not have a team to play on.

ATHLETES >> At the pro level right now, you're going to start having fans follow you on Twitter, Facebook, and Instagram—and come to your games. You've got to show a lot of respect for those fans.

At the Super Cup in Sweden, you can see the players hugging fans afterward and just spending a great deal of time with them following the game. It is so moving to see little girls absolutely glowing as they get autographs from their favorite heroines. As a coach, it makes you proud to see your players making such a connection with the fans; and as a fan, that moment of genuine engagement can mean so, so much.

Don't ever take your fans for granted and don't ever think you are above meeting them, snapping photos, or shaking hands. Your supporters are a huge part of who you are as a player.

ATHLETES >> When Christen Press got drafted in the first round and had to share the front position with Abby Wambach, we talked about how important it was for her to give respect to the senior players who have paid their dues. The reason why she's playing at the level she is, is because these players paved the way for her. It is tremendously important when a rookie comes into a team that she gives the respect to the veteran players because of their experience and the ways that they can guide younger players on and off the field. It could be the turning point in a player growing as an athlete by being willing to be mentored. —*Ziad*

SPORTSMANSHIP

GOOD SPORTSMANSHIP starts with respect for one's teammates, opponents, coaches, and officials. A Level-5 **COMPLETE ATHLETE** demonstrates good sportsmanship by:

- Playing by the rules and never cheating
- Acknowledging and encouraging her teammates
- Accepting responsibility for her own mistakes
- Never arguing with the officials
- Winning and losing with grace

As a professional soccer player, you must always remember that you are not the only player on the team. Even if you're a star player, you can't win a game all by yourself. Demonstrate good sportsmanship by giving credit to your teammates and your coaches when you win a game. You should also acknowledge that the other team was a formidable opponent.

ATHLETES >> One of the best examples of sportsmanship at the professional level was the Women's World Cup final between Japan and the United States. It was supposed to be a great match-up, but the game was over by half-time with a score of 4-1. What was so amazing, though, was that the Japanese team never argued with the referees or with one another. They stayed respectful and they continued to encourage one another as a team. After the game, they shook hands and didn't act angry. They were being watched by their country and by the whole world, and they absolutely shone in terms of what real sportsmanship looks like. They were an example for every team, every player, and every coach to learn from. It was amazing to watch. –*Walid and Ziad*

TEAMWORK

A soccer player who reaches the professional ranks will likely join a team that is already a tight-knit family. She is going to need to earn the trust of her new teammates and maintain that trust using the skills she has learned up to this point.

COMPLETE ATHLETE

JOIN THE CONVERSATION!
Download the Complete Athlete app now!

PROFESSIONALISM

As a Level-5 **COMPLETE ATHLETE**, a soccer player simply needs to be the **PROFESSIONAL** that she is being paid to be by representing her team and her sport admirably. In addition to the list of dos and don'ts presented in Level 4, a professional athlete must learn how to speak to the media correctly and in a way that presents her team in a good light.

ATHLETES >> At this level, every player has to understand that it's not about the name on the back of the jersey; it's about the name on the front of the jersey. Whenever you're doing an interview or doing any charity work or involved in community activities, you've got to always remember that you're representing a club, you're representing your whole roster of that year, you're representing the tradition that club set up in that community, and it's not about you. It's about the team.

It's really important for the players to control their emotions, especially during an interview after a heart-breaking loss. Know that there are thousands, if not tens of or hundreds of thousands, of people watching that interview. They are waiting for you to see what you are going to say. Are you going to blame a teammate for costing you the game, or are you going to do just the opposite? Are you going to say, "We gave it everything and today just wasn't our day," or are you going to start pointing fingers? Remember that every single thing you say or do at that level is representing your team, your traditions, and your community. *–Ziad*

LEADERSHIP

Whether or not a student-athlete moves into professional level play, the **LEADERSHIP** skills she has developed over the years will continue to benefit her as she leaves college. In corporate America, as on a soccer team, a strong, confident leader can inspire a team to accomplish goals that they can't accomplish on their own. This is one of the many reasons why many companies hire former athletes.

A former player may consider coaching, moving up from introductory levels to higher levels of coaching. According to the U.S. Bureau of Labor Statistics, employment of coaches is expected to increase much faster than the average for all occupations through 2022. Nonetheless, there will be a lot of competition for college and professional coaching jobs.

The athlete who has developed strong leadership skills over the years will be a much more attractive candidate, because she will already possess the following:

- Excellent communication skills that allow her to effectively teach and convey information to her team
- The ability to make quick decisions, especially during games and other high-pressure situations
- Effective interpersonal skills that allow her to relate to her players
- Negotiation skills that allow her to solve problems in the best interest of everyone involved

ATHLETES >> When you're in that little tunnel with the opposing team lining up next to you, and the referees are right in front of you, and you are waiting for them to give you the green light to step on the field because the TV is going to start, and it's going to be live feeding, and this is when the TV had the cameras on the team in that tunnel ... imagine that you are standing right across from your opponent and channel that energy into your mind, your body, your eyes, and your voice.

Recently, just before a big Premier League game between Arsenal and Leicester on television, there were cameras on both teams and about 80,000 fans in attendance waiting for the teams to step onto the field. All the players were trying to look sharp in front of the camera and put a smile on their faces, but when that green light was given for both teams to walk on the field, Arsenal captain's whole demeanor changed. In an instant it went from, "Yeah, we have a big game right now, lads," to, "Come on, men, we're going to war and we are representing all of our fans today." It was an amazing moment to witness the leader forget about everything going on around him and shift his mind to a place where he knew he had to get his players in that state of mind.
–Walid and Ziad

CAMILLE LEVIN >> *I ended up going to Europe when I first entered the pros—a lot of Americans do. I was drafted by a Swedish team, and I was fortunate because a lot of Swedes speak English very well, so it wasn't too big of an adjustment. But it can be kind of overwhelming at first to be living in a new country and not speaking the language, trying to learn a new culture, understanding how people work there, and how things work there in general. At the end of the day, though, I was there for soccer, so when you're on the field, it doesn't matter where you are or where you came from. There are different play styles and different approaches, but we* were all there to play soccer. When I was on the field, I was confident in what I was doing and I was in my happy place. Wherever you are, at the end of the day, you're on a soccer field with a ball and your team. It doesn't matter what language they're speaking or what culture differences there are—ultimately, you're all there for the same reason. That is a pretty neat thing about the sport and how universal it is.

 ## PREPARATION

PREPARATION refers to off-the-field activities, such as practicing skills, eating right, staying hydrated, getting enough rest, and mentally preparing for a game or practice. A **COMPLETE ATHLETE** prepares to perform on the field of play by continuously improving on the following:

PRACTICE

NUTRITION

HYDRATION

RECOVERY

MENTALITY

PRACTICE

If you have become a Level-5 **COMPLETE ATHLETE**, you may already be playing soccer professionally. Like at Level 4, **PRACTICE** sessions will be supervised by an elite coaching staff. Nonetheless, a professional soccer player takes full responsibility for training and practicing safely, both independently as well as with the team. She knows her body well enough to know how to push herself while at the same time minimizing the risk of injury. After all, an injured player can't play at her full potential.

A Level-5 **COMPLETE ATHLETE** continues to practice those skills she has already mastered—including the basics. In addition, she develops and practices new and innovative skills that can provide a competitive advantage for her team.

ATHLETES » I was stuck in Chicago O'Hare with a connecting-flight delay that wouldn't leave until late the next day, so I called my friend Rory Damos, coach of the Chicago Red Stars. He came and picked me up and invited me to watch the team practice, so I did. Afterward, I noticed two players who stayed afterward doing extra shots: Julie Johnston and Christen Press, both of whom had just played in the World Cup. They were probably the two players who least needed to stay after for extra work, but there they were, fresh off of winning the World Cup. Even now, at the highest point of their careers, they were still putting in the extra time—which is the reason they reached such a high level in the first place.

I coached Christen Press from the time she was at Level 1 all the way through, and she always showed up early or stayed late to take shots. That's the reason she broke the record for the most goals scored ever in Stanford history. That's why she already has 31 goals for the U.S. National Team. It goes to show you how important practice is and how it is even more important to put your own time into practices after your official practice is done. *—Walid*

NUTRITION

As a college student-athlete moves on to professional sports, **NUTRITION** continues to play a key role, not only for optimal performance on the field of play, but also for optimal health throughout life.

LEVEL-5 ATHLETE NUTRITION GUIDELINES »

Each individual has different macronutrient needs, based on height, weight, age, activity level, and genetic background. The following macronutrient guidelines are based on age and estimated activity level for a Level-5 athlete:

- 45% carbohydrate
- 35% protein
- 20% fat
- No more than 7% saturated fat
- No trans fat
- 38-40 grams of fiber per day
- No more than 150 calories per day from sugar
  (37.5 grams or 9 teaspoons)

ATHLETES » As a professional, the way you take care of yourself says everything about you. The more you put the right food in your body and stay in playing condition, the more longevity and fewer injuries you're going to have as an athlete. It tells coaches what kind of shape you are in when you come in the pre-season. Among the really great players, the common denominator is that they always take care of themselves in the off-season. They get up in the morning and work out on their own or with other players from the team, or they even hire their own conditioning coaches and nutritionists. They take care of themselves because they know how important it is for them when they show up to that first practice, to that first pre-season camp. The biggest indicator to their coaches of where they are at, their commitment to their team, and how promising their future is, is what kind of care those athletes take of their bodies in the off-season.

HYDRATION

All athletes should drink water before, during, and after practices and games.*

HOW TO MAINTAIN PROPER HYDRATION*>>

- Before exercise, drink 16–20 full ounces within the 2-hour period prior to exercise.
- During exercise, drink 4–6 full ounces.
- After exercise, replace 24 full ounces for every one pound of body weight lost during exercise.
* *Adapted from guidelines provided by the American College of Sports Medicine (ACSM)*

COMPLETE
ATHLETE

JOIN THE CONVERSATION!
Download the Complete Athlete app now!

RECOVERY

A Level-5 athlete needs to eat and drink within 30 minutes of a practice or game to make up for the calories she is burning and fluids she is using. Replenishing calories and fluids also aids in muscle **RECOVERY** and repair.

HOW TO REPLENISH CALORIES AND FLUIDS »

- Drink 24 ounces of fluid for every pound of sweat lost within a 2-hour period of a game or practice.
- Consume 30–35 grams of protein plus an equal amount of carbohydrates within the 30-minute recovery window.

SLEEP Sleep is still very important for muscle recovery and repair at this stage. Inadequate sleep will have a negative effect on athletic performance, and your body will not be able to bounce back as easily as it did when you were younger. According to the National Sleep Foundation, a Level-5 athlete should get 7–9 hours of sleep each night.

**COMPLETE
ATHLETE**

JOIN THE CONVERSATION!
Download the Complete Athlete app now!

Obviously, research cannot pinpoint the exact amount of sleep needed by a particular individual, which is why it's so important to pay attention to your own individual need for rest and recovery. One way to do this is by assessing how you feel on different amounts of sleep. For example:

· Are you productive, healthy, and happy on seven hours of sleep? Or do you need closer to nine hours of quality sleep to feel this way?
· Do you wake feeling groggy, or do you bounce out of bed ready to take on the day?
· Do you depend on caffeine to get you through the day?
· Do you feel sleepy when driving?

Experimenting with different amounts of sleep can give you a better idea of what your particular needs are for quality sleep.

ATHLETES » Finding a work-life balance is so important for professional athletes. You see it over and over: when a team travels to another city, relatives, friends, and former teammates come out to meet the players. They want to grab dinner, grab a drink, catch up—and that is wonderful! But a professional also needs to know when to say, "Thank you! It was great seeing you, but it's time for me to go now. I need to sleep before tomorrow." A common denominator among great athletes is the strength to know when to say good-bye to well-intentioned visitors, because a lack of sleep is cumulative, and when it happens in city after city where people want to hang out, it can really wear on a person who is trying to balance their social life with a professional life in which they get paid to do what they love.

MENTALITY

Being a better athlete does not necessarily mean training harder or longer. Certainly, a youth soccer player must spend time physically preparing her body to meet the demands of a practice session or game. Similarly, engaging in **MENTAL PREPARATION** can help her perform at a higher level by creating the proper mindset for either practice or a game.

At Level 5, focus remains an important part of mental preparedness. More and more elite athletes and sports programs are incorporating mindfulness, meditation, and other practices into their training regimen. According to Kristen Race, Ph.D., an expert on brain-based mindfulness solutions, "Mindfulness helps train the prefrontal cortex, the part of the brain that creates a calm and alert state of mind, which helps us stay focused, avoid distraction, and perform at our best." [1]

Practicing mindfulness is not easy, but like everything else in sports, the more you do it, the better you get at it. Dr. Race suggests the following tips for practicing mindfulness:

ENGAGE IN MINDFUL BREATHING every morning as well as before a game or practice, to create a calm and clear state of mind. Sit comfortably, close your eyes, and start to deepen your breath. Inhale fully and exhale completely. Focus on your breath entering and exiting your body. Start with five minutes and build up from there.

CONDUCT A BODY SCAN, which can release tension, quiet the mind, and bring awareness to your body in a

1. Christine Yu. "Mindfulness for Athletes: The Secret to Better Performance." Daily Burn, 10 June 2014. (http://dailyburn.com/life/fitness/mindfulness-techniques-athletes/)

systematic way. Lie down on your back, with your palms facing up and legs relaxed. Close your eyes. Start with your toes and notice how they feel. Are they tense? Are they warm or cold? Focus your attention here for a few breaths before moving on to the sole of your foot. Repeat the process as you travel from your foot to your ankle, calf, knee, and thigh. Bring your attention to your other foot and repeat the process.

Continue to move up to your hips, lower back, stomach, chest, shoulders, arms, hands, neck, and head— maintaining your focus on each body part and any sensations there. Breathe into any areas that are holding stress and try to release it.

PAY ATTENTION TO YOUR INTERNAL DIALOGUE, which can reflect—or even shape—your mental state. Instead of thinking, *"I hope I don't miss the goal,"* speak in terms of what you want to achieve; for example, *"I'm going to score a point today."*

ATHLETES » When Christen Press joined the national team, she began relying on meditation to help ready her mind to play. Her sister had attended Villanova and began to practice meditation there; she shared the techniques with Christen, and they became an important part of her preparation before each game. Christen has stated in interviews that she believes this conscious mindfulness gives her an edge to be strong and focused for big-stage games, like the Olympics qualifiers, the World Cup qualifiers, and World Cup matches.

FITNESS

Level 5 is the highest level of soccer. At this level, your own dedication to **FITNESS** will not only make you stronger than your opponents, but also more flexible, more explosive, faster, and healthier.

All of the exercises and tests below have been described in earlier sections. Your goal is to compete against your previous scores and always strive to improve.

LOWER-BODY STRENGTH

UPPER-BODY STRENGTH

CORE STRENGTH

LOWER-BODY STRENGTH

At Level 5, as a professional, you are at the top of your game physically; you are stronger, more explosive, healthier, and better balanced than ever before. You are staying fit during crucial practices, getting more reps because of it, and seeing the difference on the pitch. If you keep your fitness and health during practice and games, it may be the difference in making a higher salary or being chosen to play for a national team. Stronger legs have made you faster to the point of contact, and you are now out-jumping your opponent for free balls in the air or winning slide tackles. Single-leg squats are easier, your balance is top-notch, and your jumping is exceptionally high. Congrats—you are ready for Level-5 testing and dominating any challenge!

UPPER-BODY STRENGTH

You may now be playing against players 5-10 years older than you. You may be just as skilled, but are you just as strong? National coaches will be looking at you to separate yourself from competition, so the margin for error is minuscule. At this level, decisions may come down to match-ups with other teams just as skilled, so skill may not be what is most important at some positions. You don't want to be on the bench due to your lack of strength!

COMPLETE ATHLETE

JOIN THE CONVERSATION!
Download the Complete Athlete app now!

CORE STRENGTH

You are in the best shape of your life, playing against some of the most elite players in the world, and every athlete is out to either beat you or take your job—so staying healthy can be as important as scoring a goal. This is where having a strong core can be crucial for a soccer player. You need your hips to be strong to deliver accurate, crisp passes, and your lower back needs to be able to support all the torque that comes with kicking a ball powerfully. A weakness in your core means you are likely going to be injured sooner rather than later.

COMPLETE ATHLETE

JOIN THE CONVERSATION!
Download the Complete Athlete app now!

LEVEL-5 FITNESS TEST

LOWER-BODY STRENGTH »

- 10 full-range single-leg squats on each leg
- Single-leg wall squat for at least 85 seconds
- Broad jump of 92 inches or more
- Vertical jump of 22 inches or more

UPPER-BODY STRENGTH »

- Bent-arm hold pull-up for 30 seconds
- 45 push-ups in 60 seconds

FLEXIBILITY/MOBILITY »

- Sit-and-reach test minimum of 43 centimeters
- 90/90 test is pass or fail

CORE STRENGTH/BALANCE »

- Plank for 3 minutes
- Side plank for 60 seconds on each side
- Hip-lift march with perfect form for 3 minutes
- Single-leg balance on each leg for 60 seconds
- Standing overhead 6-pound medicine-ball throw of at least 8 yards

SPEED/QUICKNESS/ENDURANCE »

- 5-10-5 shuttle run in 4.7 seconds
- 30-yard sprint in 4.5 seconds
- Beep test score 8/6-10/1 or better (number of levels/ number of shuttles completed)

5.4 TECHNIQUE

Level 5 is the highest level of technical ability, and reaching this level of soccer requires the ability to perform on the highest stage. Playing at the professional/international level will consist of many challenges and sacrifices. At this level, you are constantly under the microscope, with the pressure to perform on the biggest stage—one that few get to experience. Remember, being a **COMPLETE ATHLETE,** it is up to you to continue to master the four previous levels in order to play the game of soccer at the highest level. Understanding the tactical roles and responsibilities with players that can interchange within systems, will test your technical ability to the highest level.

Playing at the professional/international level is the greatest honor in the game of soccer. Using these technical tools and developing them to perform consistently in this environment is the final challenge on your journey to being a **COMPLETE ATHLETE**:

FOUNDATIONAL BALL SKILLS / DRIBBLING

PASSING

BALL CONTROL

BALL-STRIKING / SHOOTING

HEADING

FOUNDATIONAL BALL SKILLS / DRIBBLING

- Consistent dribbling habits on both feet to keep all abilities sharp and consistent
- Ability to read opponents' weaknesses to use your moves effectively
- Being able to perform with creative skill, speed, and change of pace with both feet, and to play either side of the field or the center
- Deception to freeze opponents with upper and lower body
- Ability to read teammates' movement, in order to penetrate opponents' open areas

PASSING

- Ability to weight balls to play to feet or lead away from pressure with both feet accurately in all areas of the field
- Driving balls with range of 50 yards plus, with both feet
- Bending the ball with appropriate weight and accuracy for service or to switch the field with both feet
- Chipping weighted balls in by reading opponents' shape and timing of teammates' runs
- Using the outside of the foot in tight areas to show quality and vision to break through opponents
- Deceptive Cryuff, heel, and flick passes to play through tight gaps to penetrate

COMPLETE
ATHLETE

JOIN THE CONVERSATION!
Download the Complete Athlete app now!

BALL CONTROL

- Using all surfaces of the feet and body from all distances on the field
- Receiving the ball at the highest level of speed with the inside or outside of both feet away from pressure
- Ability to turn with physical pressure with either foot inside or outside to beat opponent
- Ability to control the ball out of the air at full speed from 50 yards plus with both feet, either thigh, or on the chest
- Receiving to turn with the ball with physical pressure out of the air or off the bounce

BALL-STRIKING / SHOOTING

- Reading the positioning of the goalkeeper for finishing with the instep to drive inside and outside of the box with either foot
- Inside-of-the-foot finishing with both feet
- Reading the positioning of the goalkeeper to bend the ball with either foot to finish
- Chipping the goalkeeper with either foot when high off line or out of position
- Inside-of-the-foot volleys with both feet from wide service or knock-downs
- Outside-of-the-foot to beat the goalkeeper when sliding in the opposite direction
- Juggle or flick-up touch to set up volley, or timing of full-scissor kick, or over-the-head kick when the ball arrives into your body in the right way to connect on goal

HEADING

- For distance, passing or clearing over the opponents' midfield
- Flicking with timing of teammates' run
- Clearing high and wide to stop pressure
- Deceptive movement and timing to step in front or behind to lose opponent and then to snap flick across the goalkeeper to finish, or head down either side of the goalkeeper to finish
- Diving header waist-height ball at speed to clear the ball, or arrive in the area at full speed to get on the end of wide service to finish

5.5 LIFESTYLE

For student-athletes who become one of the rare few who move on to the professional level in their sport, life can sometimes feel like an open book. More people are watching them play, and they are more in the public eye than ever before. A Level-5 **COMPLETE ATHLETE** is one who continues to successfully balance all the elements in her life, including:

FAMILY

ACADEMICS

SOCIAL LIFE

ROLE MODEL

FAMILY

As a professional athlete, you should continue to strive to maintain positive relationships with your **FAMILY** members by:

- Setting aside a specific day and time each week to talk to your family by phone
- Communicating regularly via e-mail or text messaging
- Attending special family events whenever possible
- Reassuring your family that they are still an important part of your life
- Remembering that you're in the public eye and always striving to make your family proud

ATHLETES » Whenever we do a Q&A with professional athletes for our younger players, one of the most common questions we hear is, "What do you do when you have a bad game? How do you react?"

The common denominator for the majority of the pros is that they make a separation between the game and their lives. After a game, they go home and spend time with their partners or parents or siblings—whatever their family situation is, they spend time with those people they love the most to help detach emotionally from the game.

As we tell them, there is nothing they can do to change the outcome now except to look forward to practicing and fixing whatever didn't go right. But they have to have that positive retreat from the pressure of the sport; don't bring the negative vibe of feeling like a failure, or that you let people down, into your family space. Just knowing when it's time to enjoy the company of family, and when it's time to get back on the parctice field, goes a long way in helping a professional play soccer at the highest level for a long time.

ACADEMICS

As a Level-5 **COMPLETE ATHLETE**, you should have earned your degree at college. As a professional athlete, you should take advantage of continuing education opportunities. For example, some sports organizations provide signing bonuses that include money just for school. Even if you're not provided with education money, you should strive to expand your mind in new and different ways.

For example, business classes can help you later in life when you retire from sports. Taking classes just for fun, such as a foreign-language class or an art class, can provide an opportunity to develop creative skills. Yoga classes can help you reduce stress and even improve your performance on the field of play.

ATHLETES >> The women's professional league draft is in December, so we have a lot of players who opt out of school in December to get drafted—which means they don't finish their last semester of school. Many of them end up getting drafted, playing their season, and then returning to finish their last semester during the off-season.

That is so important because, at the end of the day, they have invested so much time in school and they are so close to finishing that it would be a waste not to. Even if they get drafted, they can still go back and finish their degree, and we always encourage them to do so. Otherwise, what do you do if your career is cut short due to injury, or when you choose to retire? You've got to have that degree to think about transitioning to life outside of soccer. *–Walid and Ziad*

SOCIAL LIFE

As a Level-5 **COMPLETE ATHLETE**, you should continue to maintain a supportive **SOCIAL LIFE**. Make time for your friends when you can, and always strive to be a true friend. At the same time, be careful who you associate with, because you will be judged by the company you keep.

ATHLETES » One time, we were running a camp with Paul Burns, who back then was the assistant coach for Newcastle United in England in the Premier League. He said, "What other element do you add to the most important elements that make a soccer player? What makes a soccer player is their technical ability, tactical ability and psychological and physical ability, but in the Premier League, one of the most important things that we look for is your lifestyle."

When players begin signing contracts and making money, they often don't know what to do with the sudden fame and fortune, and their entire lifestyle changes. Their social life becomes all about going out, partying, having a good time—and then they end up coming to games unprepared. It affects the way they play, as well as their mental game.

Who you choose to hang around with and how you choose to spend your time makes even more difference now than it did when you were in school, because now you don't have your parents to hold you accountable or the fear of losing a scholarship to help you make good choices. Pick the right friends, surround yourself with the right people, pay attention to the older players who have learned how to find the balance, and that will be the key to being truly successful.

ROLE MODEL

These days, everyone has a cell phone with a camera. For a professional athlete—or anyone in the public eye—one mistake can be broadcast internationally in a matter of moments. Remember that young people are looking up to you. Be a good role-model citizen by behaving well and by engaging in charity work and community service.

KASSI MCCLUSKIE >> *Now that my profession is as a coach, I appreciate even more how important it is to have good role models in women's sports. Mentoring is so important for both the older and younger players with whom I work. As a coach, I love having a big sister/little sister pairing with the teams in our club so that players at lower levels are matched with players at the higher levels. The girls are encouraged to go to one another's games to cheer each other on, or to make encouragement cards and signs before big games. Unfortunately, I still don't think there are enough female role models out there in the world of sports, so it is really fantastic for younger girls to have older girls they can watch and learn from in a personal, one-on-one manner. In the same way, it is a wonderful leadership learning opportunity for older players to interact with the younger girls and think carefully not only about how to cheer for them and work on skills, but also about how they talk and act. I think it is a positive experience for everyone.*

MIA HAMM

When a player reaches the pros, certain things are completely new, but other things remain exactly the same as they have always been. For example, you are going to be up against better players than ever before and new playing styles you may not have encountered in the past—especially if you're playing internationally. That means your game always has to be evolving and adapting, and you can't think, "I've arrived! I know all I need to know." Now it is more important than ever to keep improving and practicing and growing. Even as you look to make the most of your own talents and unique skills, be sure you understand how those things fit in the team dynamic.

When I was growing up, there weren't really many girls' soccer programs, so I ended up playing on mostly coed teams that didn't have many girls on them. They were really just mostly boys' teams. As a result, I learned to be competitive in a different kind of way, and I've always been grateful for how those experiences shaped me to make me a tougher player. I know other women who had similar experiences. Sometimes, girls on coed teams were told, "Oh, don't play so hard. You don't need to work as hard as you do." My parents never said anything like that, but I know plenty of women who did hear things like that. When I got to college, however, the message was always, "Don't you want to see how good you can be? Don't you think you owe that to yourself?" I loved that message, and I think it is as true at Level 1 as it is at Level 5, and every level in between. Working hard is not just for a certain few on the team—it's for everyone.

One of the ways I let my teammates on the U.S. National Team know I cared about them was by working hard and giving my all every single practice, every single game, every single minute of the day. I wanted them to know that I was thinking about our team when we were together as well as when we were apart. That meant that I showed up to camp as fit as possible, instead of letting my fitness lapse in the off-season; and I knew they were doing the same for me. And I was committed to continuing to learn. I learned something every single day because I never wanted to stop growing and improving as a player and as a person. The more invested I was in getting better in every aspect of my professional and personal life, the better person and player I was going to be. That's what makes an athlete a **COMPLETE ATHLETE**.

COMPLETE
ATHLETE

JOIN THE CONVERSATION!
Download the Complete Athlete app now!

APPENDIX 1:
AN OVERVIEW OF SOCCER

Soccer has a very interesting history. Believe it or not, there is evidence that a game similar to soccer was played in China during the 2nd and 3rd centuries BC! Ancient Roman and Greek warriors also played a form of soccer to help them prepare for battle.

During the 8th century AD, the first soccer games were played in Britain. These games were very violent. Injury and even death occurred in nearly every game. For this reason, soccer was banned in England by King Edward in 1365. Anyone who was caught playing soccer was thrown into prison.

Soccer was banned by many other kings and queens of England who came after King Edward. However, this did not stop people from playing the game. For many centuries, there were no universally accepted rules for soccer. Different forms of the game were played in different areas of Great Britain.

SOCCER RULES ESTABLISHED

In 1863, the first-ever association for soccer was founded in England. It was called the Football Association, or FA, because in Europe, soccer is called football. Representatives from schools and clubs around Great Britain got together and established the first set of common rules for soccer matches.

Now that soccer had a standard set of rules, other European countries began to play the game. Many club teams were formed during the late 1800s and early 1900s in countries like Denmark, the Netherlands, New Zealand, Argentina, Belgium, Chile, Switzerland, Italy, Uruguay, Germany, Hungary, and Finland.

In May 1904 in Paris, France, the governing body for worldwide soccer was established. It was named the *Fédération Internationale de Football Association*, or FIFA (FEE-fah) for short. In English, it means the International Federation of Association Football. FIFA is responsible for overseeing international competitions. FIFA also organizes the World Cup and the Women's World Cup.

WOMEN IN SOCCER

How long have women been playing soccer? Well, evidence shows that women played in the violent soccer games of old England! However, the Football Association's rules of 1863 established that the game was for men only. Nonetheless, women in England and Scotland played in informal soccer matches through the end of the 19th century and into the 20th century.

In Europe, women's soccer leagues began around 1930, and international competitions started in the 1950s. In the United States, women's soccer was confined to gym class, informal pick-up games, and college intramural competition until around the 1970s.

By 1981, there were almost 100 varsity programs established in NCAA women's soccer, and even more club teams. By 2001, Division-1 women's college soccer tournaments started with 64 teams, compared to only 32 teams for the men. Teams at UNC, UConn, Notre Dame, UCLA, and Penn State became regular contenders for the national title.

After college, some of the women on the college teams became professional soccer players. They joined the United States Women's National Team (USWNT), which represents the United States of America in international soccer competitions.

Today, the United States is considered the top country in the world for women's soccer, both in terms of participation and in international competition. The United States Women's National Team has won three World Cups, four Olympic gold medals, and one Olympic silver medal.

RULES OF SOCCER

The rules of soccer are based on the 17 Laws of the Game. The laws were developed by FIFA, and are maintained by the International Football Association Board (IFAB). These laws govern any professional or international match played.

The 17 Laws of the Game were created to ensure fairness when people play soccer. They also govern the field of play, the size of the soccer ball, and what referees are supposed to do during a game.

Following is an overview of what you need to know in order to play soccer at a beginner's level. If you would like to read the latest version of the Laws of the Game, go to FIFA's website at *www.fifa.com*.

THE SOCCER FIELD

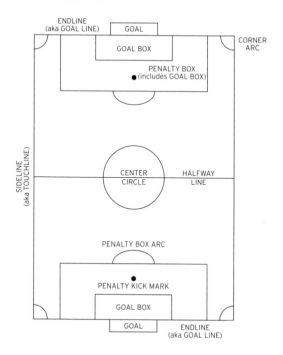

Soccer is played on a rectangular field. The **GOAL LINES** on are the short sides of the rectangle. The **SIDELINES**, or touchlines, are on the long sides of the rectangle. The goal lines and sidelines form the boundaries of the field of play.

The soccer field is divided into two halves by the **HALFWAY LINE**. The **CENTER CIRCLE** is marked at the midpoint of the halfway line.

A **GOAL AREA** is at each end of the field. **THE PENALTY AREA** includes the penalty box and the goal box.

The following areas of the soccer field must be marked:

- Touchlines/Sidelines
- Goal lines and goal areas
- Halfway line
- Center circle
- Penalty areas
- Arcs and spots
- Corner arcs

In addition, a flag post should be placed at each corner of the field. Also a **GOAL** should be placed on the center of each goal line. It needs to have two goalposts and a crossbar on top.

The main objective of soccer is to score a goal with any part of the body **EXCEPT** the arms and hands. A goal is scored if the ball crosses the goal line between the two goalposts and under the crossbar. The side that scores the most goals wins. If both teams have the same number of goals at the end of the match, it is considered a draw—even if neither of them scored a goal.

Soccer is played by two teams. Each team must have at least 7 players but no more than 11 players. A soccer match lasts for 90 minutes, played in two equal halves of 45 minutes.

A **KICKOFF** starts a soccer game. It also restarts the game at the second half or after a goal is scored. A coin toss determines which team kicks off the ball at the beginning of the match. During the kickoff, only two players are allowed inside the center circle—the one kicking and the one receiving the ball.

The **SOCCER BALL IS OUT OF BOUNDS** if it crosses the goal line or touchline either on the ground or in air. The team that DID NOT have possession of the ball before it went out of bounds is awarded a throw-in. While taking a **THROW-IN**, a player must release the ball with both hands simultaneously and keep both feet firmly planted on the ground.

FOULS AND PENALTIES

The most common fouls in soccer are:

- Kicking, tripping, pushing, or charging another player
- Hitting or attempting to hit any member of the opposite team
- Using your hand on the ball (except the goalkeeper)
- Using excessive force in defending an opponent

The **REFEREE** is in charge of calling fouls. He or she also strives to prevent multiple fouls by the same player by using **YELLOW AND RED CARDS.**

A **YELLOW CARD** is a warning. Two yellow cards are equivalent to a **RED CARD.** A player who receives a red card is sent to the bench, and her team cannot replace her. This means her teammates must continue the game with one less player.

A **FREE KICK** restarts a play after a foul is committed and is usually taken from the spot where the foul happened. A free kick can either be **DIRECT**, where the player may score directly, or **INDIRECT**, where another player must touch the ball before a goal can be scored.

A **PENALTY KICK** is awarded to the opposite team when a player commits a foul inside her team's penalty area. The kick is taken from the penalty spot, and all the players except the kicker and the goalkeeper must be outside the penalty area and penalty arc.

A **GOAL KICK** is awarded when the offensive team plays the ball out of bounds over the defensive team's goal line. After the ball is out of play, the defender or goalkeeper may place the ball anywhere within the goal box and kick the ball back into play.

A **CORNER KICK** is awarded to the attacking team if an opposing player is the last to touch the ball before it goes out of bounds on the goal line. The attacking team resumes play by placing the ball in the corner arc nearest to where it crossed the goal line.

APPENDIX 2:
SPORTS NUTRITION GUIDELINES
FOR ATHLETES

All of the Complete Athlete *sports nutrition guidelines were provided by Courtney M. Sullivan, founder of Nutrition for Body and Mind. Sullivan is a Registered Dietitian certified by the Academy of Nutrition and Dietetics, and a Certified Personal Trainer recognized by the National Academy of Sports Medicine. Below are more detailed guidelines as well as suggested meals and recipes developed by Sullivan.*

Nutrition is key to enhancing your athletic performance.

Young athletes with inadequate diets may have insufficient fuel for workouts, and/or nutrient deficiencies that can lead to fatigue, a compromised immune system, and possible injury. All of these will be reflected in their performance, regardless of their determination.

Proper intake of macronutrients and micronutrients is vital to enhance sports performance. Critical micronutrients include calcium, iron, folate, vitamin B6, and zinc.

CALCIUM

Poor calcium intake can lead to decreased bone mass and increased risk for stress fractures and possible bone-related injuries. The adequate intake of calcium for children who are 9-18 years old is 1,300 milligrams per day. Women who are 25-50 years old require 1,000-1,200 milligrams per day. Women who are pregnant or lactating require 1,500 milligrams per day.

IRON

Important for its oxygen-carrying capacity, iron also plays a major role in the energy metabolism of carbohydrates, proteins, and fats. Young athletes with iron-deficiency anemia are at risk of performance inhibition as evidenced by fatigue, impaired immune function, and/or impaired cognitive reasoning. Foods that are rich in iron include red meat and enriched cereals and grains, coupled with fruits and vegetables that are high in vitamin C, which aids in iron absorption.

FOLATE AND VITAMIN B6

Both are critical for amino-acid metabolism. Good sources of both are enriched grain products and assorted animal products. Spinach, broccoli, lentils, and asparagus are also rich sources of folate. A vitamin-B-complex deficiency can lead to fatigue, muscle soreness, and loss of cognitive function.

ZINC

Athletes are at risk of zinc deficiency due to poor consumption of foods rich in this mineral. Zinc plays a role in more than 300 enzymatic reactions in the body. It is also critical for wound healing, tissue growth and maintenance, and immune function. Dietary protein enhances zinc absorption and plays an important role in muscle recovery.

MACRONUTRIENTS

An increase in energy expenditure will require an increase in the intake of carbohydrates, protein, and fats.

However, you should consult with a Registered Dietitian to inquire about your customized macronutrient needs, which will be based on your height, weight, age, activity level, and gender.

Activity level is measured by the time (how long you exercise), type (sport or training program you're currently in), intensity (low, moderate, or high), and frequency (how often you perform this exercise/training). After determining these factors, your estimated calorie burn will be established.

Current research is showing that an increasing percentage of athletes are not consuming enough total calories, as well as total carbohydrates, in comparison to the amount of calories they burn. Fluid intake is often inadequate as well, which alters the hydration status of young athletes. Therefore, it is very important to practice a pre- and post-workout nutrition regimen and rehydration program.

CARBOHYDRATES

For athletes, poor carbohydrate intake results in inadequate glycogen stores and fatigue, which compromises sports performance and forces your body to break down its own protein stores for fuel (through a process called gluconeogenesis). Carbohydrate is the preferred fuel source for athletic performance. Carbohydrate needs are based on body weight and intensity of activity.

- 3-5 grams of carbohydrates per kilogram of body weight for very light intensity training
- 5-8 grams of carbohydrates per kilogram of body weight for moderate or heavy training
- 8-9 grams of carbohydrates per kilogram of body weight for pre-game loading (24-48 hours prior)
- 1.7 grams of carbohydrate per kilogram of body weight for post-event refueling (within 2-3 hours)

PROTEIN

Protein is essential for athletes, with its role in muscle-building and lean-muscle maintenance, repair, and/or gain. It is important to note that an adequate protein intake and inadequate total calorie intake will inhibit protein balance, and can still cause lean muscle breakdown. It is critical that athletes consume adequate total calories and protein to avoid this problem and maintain a healthy body weight. Vegetarians and vegans should be mindful of consuming adequate plant proteins. On the other end, consuming excess protein can lead to dehydration (it puts strain on the kidneys), weight gain (your body will store as fat the excess protein that is not utilized), and calcium loss.

- Athletes who have just begun a training program need 1-1.5 grams of protein per kilogram of body weight
- Athletes participating in endurance sports require 1.2-1.4 grams of protein per kilogram of body weight

FAT

Fat is essential for light-to-moderate intensity exercise and for absorption of the fat-soluble vitamins. Low-fat diets are not encouraged. Adequate heart healthy fats such as monounsaturated and polyunsaturated fats should make up 20-30% of your total calories. Lowering the amount of saturated fat and trans fat (the unhealthy fats) is highly encouraged. Ideally, your diet should consist of <7% of total calories from saturated fat and preferably no trans fat.

FLUID

Maintaining proper fluid balance is critical to athletic performance and avoiding early fatigue and heat exhaustion. Signs of dehydration include dark urine, small urine output, muscle cramps, increased heart rate, headaches, nausea, and vomiting.

- Be sure to consume 16-24 ounces of fluid for every pound lost via sweat during exercise.
- For activities that are less than 60 minutes, hydrate with water.
- For activities that are greater than 60 minutes, hydrate with a sports beverage containing 6-8% carbohydrates to replete electrolytes and energy.

GENERAL GUIDELINES

- All athletes should consume five or more balanced meals spread throughout the day, every 3-4 hours. Eating every 3 hours helps to maintain your metabolic rate, lower body fat percentage, lower serum lipid levels (cholesterol), decrease stress hormone production, lower insulin response, and improve glucose tolerance (especially if you are prediabetic, are diabetic currently, or have diabetes in your family history).
- Meals should be eaten 2-3 hours before practice or games, and snacks eaten 1-1 $\frac{1}{2}$ hours before practice or games.

- Eat when you're hungry to prevent lean-muscle breakdown and stop when you're full to prevent being sluggish. Listen to your intuitive eating cues, which help to do the following:

  — Maintain blood sugar and insulin control
  — Regulate appetite
  — Improve concentration
  — Gain lean-muscle mass
  — Enhance muscle in the recovery process (i.e., repairing and rebuilding of muscles)

- Eat breakfast within 30 minutes of waking up to prevent lean-muscle breakdown, increase energy and concentration, and maintain good blood sugar control. Choose whole grains, fresh fruit, and lean protein.
- Eat well-balanced meals and snacks, consisting of carbohydrates, lean proteins, and heart healthy fats.
- Drink a protein shake or eat a snack or meal that has equal amounts of protein and carbohydrates within 30 minutes after a workout.
- Choose fresh, whole foods when possible, instead of processed foods that are packaged or refined, to increase nutritional value. Especially avoid foods that are high in sugar or trans fats.

MEAL PLANNING

- **BREAKFAST »** This is the most important meal of the day so don't skip it! You are coming from an overnight fast and will wake up with low blood sugar (by default). Breakfast literally means to "break the fast." You need to focus on eating breakfast within 30 minutes of waking up to prevent lean-muscle breakdown, increase energy and concentration, and maintain good blood-sugar control.

Start your morning with 8-12 ounces of water with a squeeze of lemon wedge to rehydrate and reduce stomach acidity. Choose whole grains, fresh fruit, and lean protein. Although many breakfast choices are focused around carbohydrates, it is important to include a good source of protein for satiety and lean-muscle gain or maintenance.

EXAMPLE BREAKFAST MEAL >> 1-2 scrambled eggs (cage-free preferred), 1 slice of whole grain toast with avocado (spread on top of toast). Add a side of sliced tomatoes and a cup of low-fat cottage cheese (for added protein, as needed). If you're trying to gain weight, adding a protein shake is also ideal with breakfast.

- **SNACK >>** Choose a snack consisting of lean protein, fresh fruit, and a whole-grain carbohydrate. You can add essential, heart-healthy fat as needed.

EXAMPLE MID-MORNING SNACK MEAL >> One medium-sized organic apple (i.e., size of a tennis ball) with 2 tablespoons of natural almond butter or peanut butter and 1 cup of nonfat or low-fat plain Greek yogurt. Optional: Add sprinkled cinnamon and $1/2$ cup blueberries to mix with your yogurt.

- **LUNCH >>** Eat a well-balanced meal, consisting of carbohydrates (whole grains, not refined white flours or sugars) and lean proteins, with a side of fresh or steamed vegetables and heart-healthy fats (omega-3s).

EXAMPLE LUNCH MEAL >> 3-4 ounces of boneless, skinless lean chicken breast; $1/2$-1 cup cooked brown rice; and a side (~1 cup) of steamed mixed vegetables or green vegetable of choice (e.g., broccoli, asparagus, brussels sprouts, zucchini, etc.). Add a piece of fresh fruit, such as a medium-sized orange (size of tennis ball) on the side.

- **SNACK »** Choose a snack consisting of a lean protein, a fresh vegetable, and a whole-grain carbohydrate. Avoid consuming foods high in fat, or excessive amounts of fiber or protein, before your training practice or game, because these foods are slow-digesting. Your body needs foods that are higher in carbohydrates, which yield readily available energy for working muscles and which also contain a high nutrient/water density to increase hydration.

   EXAMPLE AFTERNOON SNACK MEAL » 1 slice of whole grain toast with a spread of hummus (1-2 tablespoons); 2 thin slices of turkey, with sliced cucumber and tomato on top. You can eat this open face or add another piece of whole grain toast for additional carbohydrates. This depends on your current age, macronutrient needs, and training regimen.

- **DINNER »** Eat a well-balanced meal consisting of carbohydrates (whole grains, not refined white flours or sugars) and lean proteins; also add fresh or steamed vegetables and heart-healthy fats (omega-3s).

   EXAMPLE DINNER MEAL » 3-4 ounces of lean protein (e.g., fish, chicken, turkey, etc.), $1/2$-1 cup cooked quinoa or baked/sweet potato with the skin, and a side salad (e.g., kale/spinach/or mixed greens with chopped tomato, garbanzo or kidney beans, shredded carrots, chopped broccoli, avocado, feta cheese, and a light balsamic vinaigrette).

POST-WORKOUT (WITHIN 30 MINUTES) >> Consume a protein shake or balanced intake of protein and carbohydrates to repair your muscles overnight and restore glycogen that was used during your practice or game, so that you are prepared to get after it tomorrow! (See the protein-shake recipes that follow for recovery nutrition.)

· **NIGHTTIME (BEFORE BED) SNACK >>** The myths that you should not eat after 7 PM or that you should not eat 2 hours before bed do not apply to you! You are an athlete and therefore you need to fuel your body properly to optimize your athletic performance.

EXAMPLE NIGHTTIME SNACK MEAL >> 1-2 tablespoons of almond butter or natural peanut butter, with $^1/_2$ cup organic raspberries or strawberries on the side. Optional: Add 1 cup nonfat plain Greek yogurt.

HYDRATION

- 14-22 ounces (2+ cups) 2 hours before exercise
- 8 ounces 10-20 minutes before exercise
- 6-8 ounces every 15-20 minutes during practice
- 16-24 ounces (2-3 cups) for every 1 pound lost within 2 hours after practice
- Sodium (Na) - 0.5-0.7 g/L in exercise lasting >1 hour (500 mg Na/hour for distance runners/heavy sweaters) - Increased risk of hyponatremia (low sodium can have dangerous effects on the body)
* Drink fluids with carbohydrates and electrolytes if exercise is longer than 1 hour, for improved performance and decreased fatigue.

Consume 24 ounces of fluid for every pound lost via sweat. Pay attention to internal cues (e.g., headaches) or external cues (e.g., urine color) to monitor hydration status. If you have a headache, you are most likely already >10% dehydrated. Your urine should be light yellow color or clear. If it is dark yellow or black, you are dehydrated and need to increase your fluids (and overall electrolytes, including sodium, potassium, calcium, and magnesium) drastically.

PHYSICAL / MENTAL EFFECTS OF DEHYDRATION

- Decreased muscle strength, speed, stamina, energy, cognitive processes
- Increased risk of injury

BENEFITS OF ADEQUATE FLUIDS

- Decreased heart rate, perceived exertion
- Increased stroke volume, cardiac output, skin blood flow, and improved athletic performance

ADDITIONAL TIPS AND TRICKS

AVOID "BOTTOM-HEAVY DIETS." This is defined as eating 2/3 of your total daily caloric intake in the after-noon or evening (anytime 3PM to 10PM). The timing of your meals will affect your body composition.

For example, studies show that an athlete who consumes a "bottom-heavy diet" will have a higher body-fat percentage than another athlete who consumes his or her meals throughout the day every 3-4 hours (even if both athletes are consuming the same total calories and following the same training regimen). You need to eat to fuel your body when your body needs the energy for optimal metabolism, for lean muscle gain, and to optimize performance. You may be skilled in soccer, but mastering your nutrition will help take you to the next level!

AVOID PACKAGED, PROCESSED, AND REFINED FOODS THAT ARE HIGH IN SUGAR OR TRANS FAT. These foods are high in preservatives and artificial ingredients that our bodies do not process well and may cause an upset stomach. These foods may provide convenience and quick energy, but they will ultimately lead to a "crash" or feeling of fatigue about 1 hour after consumption due to the quick rise and fall effect of your blood-sugar levels.

Artificial trans-fatty acids are an unhealthy fat that is added to foods to increase their shelf life (how long they are "safe" to eat). Be sure to look at the ingredient list below the nutrition facts label for "partially or fully hydrogenated oils," which means there is trans fat in the product and therefore you should avoid it. Trans fat raises your LDL (bad cholesterol) and lowers your HDL (good cholesterol), which can increase your risk of heart disease, stroke, and type II diabetes.

MACRONUTRIENTS	HEALTHY FOODS FOR LEAN-MUSCLE GAIN
CARBOHYDRATES	Fresh and dried fruits, fresh vegetables (peas, corn, potatoes topped with extra virgin olive oil), whole-grain breads, cornbread, multigrain muffins, bagels, brown/wild/jasmine rice, pasta/gluten-free pasta, cereal, steel-cut oatmeal, granola
PROTEINS	Eggs, chicken, turkey, fish, tuna, salmon, lean beef, pork tenderloin, Greek yogurt, milk (or nondairy high protein substitutes), beans, soybeans, nuts, nut butters, seeds, seed butters
FATS	Nuts and seeds (flaxseeds, chia seeds, hemp seeds, pumpkin seeds, etc.) olives, hummus, avocados, guacamole, oils (olive, canola, flaxseed, grapeseed, coconut, etc.) cheese

TIMING OF MEALS (FOR LEVELS 1-5) >> Eating smaller and more frequent meals is ideal for proper digestion, metabolism, and lean-muscle weight gain. Eating frequently yields high energy and stable blood sugar levels. Waiting too long between meals can lead to lean-muscle breakdown and weight loss. Athletes with poor nutrition are more prone to injury, especially during periods of growth and development or when their bones are strengthening or becoming more dense.

NUTRITION REGIMEN: NIGHT BEFORE GAME DAY

Avoid greasy or fried foods that are high in fat. Avoid high amounts of sugar, or refined carbohydrates, which can also make you feel sluggish. "Carb loading" is not necessary. Instead, eat a balanced meal containing lean protein, whole grain carbohydrates, and steamed vegetables. Add a protein shake for dessert (if needed).

MACRONUTRIENT SUGGESTIONS

CARBOHYDRATES >> Higher fiber foods (i.e., lower Glycemic Index), such as whole-grain bread, brown rice, whole-grain pasta, (or gluten-free versions), beans, starchy vegetables (e.g., corn, peas, potatoes), quinoa, and cereal

PROTEINS >> Chicken, turkey, or fish (e.g., wild salmon, tuna, trout, mackerel, or sardines, which are high in heart healthy omega-3 fatty acids)

FATS >> Low-fat cheese, nuts/nut butters (e.g., natural peanut butter or almond butter), avocado, seeds, oils (e.g., extra-virgin olive oil, canola oil, grapeseed oil, flaxseed oil)

VEGETABLES >> All green vegetables are preferable

PROTEINS >> Boneless, skinless chicken breast (portion: 3-6 ounces, depending on the athlete level)

CARBOHYDRATES >> Brown rice (portion: $\frac{1}{2}$-1 $\frac{1}{2}$ cups cooked, depending on the athlete level)

VEGETABLES >> Side salad with organic spinach leaves, chopped cucumbers, carrots, tomato, and a light olive oil and vinegar dressing

PROTEINS >> Ground turkey (portion: 3-6 ounces, depending on the athlete level)

CARBOHYDRATES >> Baked potato (1 medium-sized) with a dollop of low-fat Greek yogurt instead of sour cream (optional) OR brown rice and quinoa pasta (portion: $\frac{1}{2}$-1 $\frac{1}{2}$ cups cooked, depending on the athlete level)

VEGETABLES >> Steamed broccoli and mushrooms (portion: 1-2 cups, depending on the athlete level)

Avoid high fat or high protein foods the morning of game day, which are more difficult for the body to digest. Carbohydrates provide the best source of readily available energy for the body. Dairy products can be tolerated in a small amount, but when consumed in a larger amount can cause gastrointestinal discomfort (upset stomach). The body will use carbohydrates as its first source of energy.

CARBOHYDRATES >> Lower fiber foods (higher Glycemic Index), cream of rice, oatmeal with 2 grams of fiber or less, rice cereal (dry), bread (with 2 grams of fiber), or plain bagel

PROTEINS >> Eggs/egg whites, protein shakes (made with whey protein, pea protein, vegan protein, hemp protein, etc.), low-fat plain Greek yogurt

FATS >> Nuts/nut butters (e.g., peanut butter, almond butter, cashew butter, sunflower-seed butter), seeds, avocado

FRUITS >> 1 medium-sized piece of fresh fruit (e.g., banana, apple, kiwi, peach, pear, nectarine, plum, etc.)

Peanut butter (or almond butter) and jelly (or honey) sandwich on whole-wheat bread with a sliced banana

1 cup low-fat, plain Greek yogurt with $\frac{1}{2}$ cup organic blueberries, or a banana with 1 cup Rice Chex cereal. Avoid high-fiber cereals, such as Kashi, which will cause an upset stomach.

NOTE >> Greek yogurt contains 20 grams of protein per

cup and healthy probiotics, which increase immunity and aid in proper digestion. It is important to get the low-fat or nonfat version (to avoid the high saturated-fat content) and plain (to avoid the 20-22 grams of added sugar in the flavored varieties).

CAFFEINE

Caffeine has been proven to be one of the best ergogenic aids and is known to help athletes train harder and longer. Caffeine stimulates the brain and contributes to clearer thinking and greater concentration. If you like coffee or tea, consume caffeine at least 1 hour before a practice or game. **RECOMMENDATION: 1-3 MILLIGRAMS PER KILOGRAM OF BODY WEIGHT** (e.g., 200 milligrams for a 150-pound woman). Do not consume caffeine in the form of energy drinks or soda, because they have concentrated sources of sugar, which cancel out the health benefits. Coffee and green tea are natural sources of caffeine and provide a high antioxidant value (cancer-fighting). Make sure to only add a dash of honey, agave, or milk (no added sugar).

HYDRATION

- 14-22 ounces (2+ cups) 2 hours before exercise
- 8 ounces 10-20 minutes before exercise
- 6-8 ounces every 15-20 minutes during practice
- 16-24 ounces (2-3 cups) for every 1 pound lost, within 2 hours after practice
- Sodium (Na)- 0.5-0.7 g/L in exercise lasting >1 hour (500 mg Na/hour for distance runners/heavy sweaters)- Increased risk hyponatremia (low sodium can have dangerous effects on the body)

* Drink fluids with carbohydrate and electrolytes if exercise is longer than 1 hour, for improved performance and decreased fatigue

Consume 24 ounces of fluid for every 1 pound lost via sweat. Pay attention to internal cues (i.e., headaches) or external cues (i.e., urine color) to monitor hydration status. If you have a headache, you are most likely already more than 10% dehydrated. Your urine should be a light yellow color or clear. If it is dark yellow or black, you are dehydrated and need to increase your fluids (and overall electrolytes, including sodium, potassium, calcium, and magnesium) drastically.

PHYSICAL / MENTAL EFFECTS OF DEHYDRATION

- Decreased muscle strength, speed, stamina, energy, cognitive processes
- Increased risk of injury

BENEFITS OF ADEQUATE FLUIDS

- Decreased heart rate, perceived exertion
- Increased stroke volume, cardiac output, skin blood flow, and improved athletic performance

TRAVEL NUTRITION
(I.E., WHAT TO EAT WHILE ON THE ROAD)

TRAIL MIX >>

- Trader Joe's Trek Mix—sold in individual packs
- Trader Joe's raw mixed nuts
- Make your own nut trail mix with nuts (choose from almonds, pistachios, pecans, walnuts, hazelnuts, Brazil

nuts, cashews) and dried fruit (choose from cranberries, raisins, apricots, blueberries, goji berries, acai berries, mango pieces), and mix up to make your own
- 100% whole-wheat or Ezekiel 4:9 bread, with all natural peanut butter or almond butter (optional: add a sliced banana and raspberry jam)
- Granola bar (choose one that is higher in protein and carbohydrate, and low in fat, because fat is slower digesting and will not provide the quick energy you need for practice/your game)

TRAIL MIX >>

- Think Thin protein bar (gluten-free, sugar-free), Pure Protein bar, Strong and KIND bar, Greens+ protein and energy bar, Kashi granola bar (many flavors)
- Dry cereal (containing more than 3 g fiber per serving) can be eaten dry or with $1/2$ cup almond milk (examples: Kashi Go Lean, Kashi Crunch, Kashi Heart to Heart, Optimum Wheat, Optimum Slim, Shredded Wheat, Nature's Best and Nature's Path cereals, Barbara's Shredded Spoonfuls, Barbara's Puffins, and Kellogg's Special K or Rice Chex/Puffs if you're looking for a lower fiber cereal, etc.)
- Healthier chips / crackers: Reduced Guilt pita chips, Lundberg brown rice chips, Trader Joe's spicy soy flaxseed chips, vegetable chips, raisin rosemary crisps, popcorn chips, edamame crackers, bite-sized pita crackers, Blue Diamond nut thins, Kashi 7-grain crackers, high-fiber Wasa crackers, Mary's Gone gluten-free or whole-wheat crackers— mix any of these with hummus, yogurt chive dip, spinach dip, fresh salsa, or homemade guacamole
- Drinkable yogurt or Chobani or Fage or Trader Joe's single-serving Greek yogurts (if eaten within 2 hours)

- Graham crackers with a spread of almond butter or peanut butter on top
- String cheese (if eaten within 2 hours)
- Beef jerky or low-sodium turkey jerky with no nitrates or preservatives added
- Fresh portable fruit (i.e., apple, banana, pear, peach, nectarine, apricot, orange, blood orange, tangerine, plum, grapes, kiwi, berries, etc.)
- English muffin with wheat wrap with almond butter or natural peanut butter
- Multigrain, sesame seed, or 100% whole-wheat bagel with part skim mozzarella cheese or reduced-fat vegetable cream cheese (can replace with a spread of hummus or Greek yogurt if eaten within the hour or two that it was prepared)
- Cooked quinoa (place in large container and snack on with veggies)
- Yogurt-covered raisins or pretzels
- Hard-boiled eggs (if eaten within 2 hours)
- Build your own sandwich: Whole-grain dinner roll or 2 slices whole-wheat bread with lean protein (sliced turkey, chicken, or ham), 1 slice low-fat provolone cheese, mustard or hummus, lettuce, tomato, and avocado
- Almond butter and jelly/raspberry preserve sandwich on wheat bread or Ezekiel 4:9 bread for breakfast/snack on the go
- Whole-wheat pretzels (dip in all natural peanut butter for sweet and salty taste) or peanut-butter filled pretzels
- Meal replacement shakes (made with water or coconut water and whey protein, RAW protein, or Trader Joe's pure protein shakes, which have 21 grams of protein and come in chocolate or vanilla flavors).

NOTE >> Shakes require a mixer/shaker to blend the protein and beverage.

MILK PROTEINS >> Whey and casein stimulate muscle protein synthesis and prevent muscle breakdown.

HIGH-PROTEIN SHAKE RECIPES

Add natural whey protein or plant-based protein (pea protein or vegan Vega) powder to any of the following smoothies that don't already include protein powder. You can alternate between the following milks and milk substitutes: nonfat organic milk, 2% organic milk, or unsweetened versions of almond, coconut, hemp, or rice milk.

Tips to increase calories include: Use a larger serving of the nuts or nut butters and seeds or seed butters. To reduce carbohydrates, use a smaller serving of fresh or dried fruit (bananas, dates, etc.). To increase fiber and nutrients without adding calories, add more leafy greens such as kale or spinach.

THE ENERGIZER

- 8 oz. unsweetened coconut milk
- $1/_2$ banana
- 2 tablespoons hemp seeds
- 1-2 tablespoons chia seeds
- 2 dates
- Sprinkle of nutmeg

NUTRITION FACTS >> 400 calories, 16 grams fat (mono- and polyunsaturated fat), 25 grams carbohydrate, 13 grams fiber, 18 grams protein (add 10 grams protein powder as needed to make it 28 grams protein total)

PROTEIN POWER UP

- 8 oz. Silk unsweetened almond milk
- 1 scoop whey or pea protein powder
- $1/2$ c. nonfat plain Greek yogurt
- 2 tbsp. almond butter
- $1/2$ banana
- Sprinkle of cinnamon

NUTRITION FACTS » 350 calories, 20 grams fat (mono- and polyunsaturated fat), 14 grams carbohydrate, 5 grams fiber, 43 grams protein

BERRY BLAST

- 8 oz. Silk unsweetened almond milk
- $1/2$ c. blueberries
- $1/2$ c. raspberries
- $1/2$ c. blackberries
- 1 oz. raw, unsalted walnuts
- 1 tbsp. ground flaxseeds (Bob's Red Mill brand)

NUTRITION FACTS » 400 calories, 18 grams fat (mono- and polyunsaturated fat), 30 grams carbohydrate, 18 grams fiber, 10 grams protein (add 10-20 grams protein powder as needed to make it 20-30 grams protein total)

- 8 oz. unsweetened coconut milk
- 1 scoop pea protein powder
- 1 c. chopped kale
- $1/2$ c. frozen mango chunks
- 2 dates
- Slivers of fresh ginger
- Sprinkle of coconut flakes

NUTRITION FACTS >> 360 calories, 8.5 grams fat (mono- and polyunsaturated fat), 35 grams carbohydrate, 10 grams fiber, 37 grams protein

- 8 oz. coconut water
- 1-2 tsp. maca powder
- 1 tsp. turmeric powder
- $1/2$ avocado
- $1/2$ c. frozen pineapple chunks
- $1/2$ c. frozen organic blueberries
- 1 c. spinach leaves
- Touch of mint

NUTRITION FACTS >> 260 calories, 13 grams fat (monounsaturated fat), 31 grams carbohydrate, 14 grams fiber, 8 grams protein (add scoop of protein powder, 20 grams, to make 28 grams protein total)

- 8 oz. coconut water
- 1 banana
- $1/2$ pear
- $1/2$ c. chopped cucumber
- 1 c. chopped kale
- 1 fresh squeezed lemon
- Touch of cilantro
- Sprinkle of cayenne pepper (optional for spice/heat)

NUTRITION FACTS » 240 calories, 0 grams fat, 37 grams carbohydrate, 8 grams fiber, 7.5 grams protein (add scoop of protein powder, 20 grams, to make ~28 grams protein total)

ANTIOXIDANT

- 8 oz. unsweetened coconut milk
- $1/2$ c. strawberries
- $1/2$ c. blueberries
- 1 banana
- $1/2$ c. shredded carrot
- 1 c. spinach leaves
- 1 tbsp. goji berries

NUTRITION FACTS » 340 calories, 4.5 grams fat (monounsaturated fat), 45 grams carbohydrate, 25 grams fiber, 9 grams protein (add scoop of protein powder, 20 grams, to make 29 grams protein total)

- 8 oz. Silk unsweetened vanilla almond milk
- 1 scoop vanilla whey protein powder
- 1 tbsp. cacao powder
- $1/_2$ banana
- 2 dates
- 1 oz. cashews
- Sprinkle of cinnamon and nutmeg

NUTRITION FACTS » 375 calories, 20 grams fat (monounsaturated fat), 30 grams carbohydrate, 12 grams fiber, 35 grams protein

MEET THE TEAM

WALID AND ZIAD KHOURY have become two of the most recognizable faces and personalities on the sidelines of youth soccer fields all over the nation. They are founders of national powerhouse Slammers Fútbol Club, which has consistently been ranked as one of the top 5 clubs in the nation for the past 15 years. Walid and Ziad have developed some of the best players for all levels, both domestically and internationally.

The Khoury brothers have guided Slammers Fútbol Club to four Elite Club National League (ECNL) national championships, four US Youth Soccer Association national championships, four US Club Soccer national championships, and three Manchester United world championships. In 2012 and 2016, Slammers Fútbol Club was awarded the ECNL Overall Club Championship, one of the most prestigious national awards in youth soccer, which recognizes outstanding performance in competition in every age group throughout the club.

Their teams have won every major tournament in the United States. Together, the Khoury brothers have coached more than 400 athletes who went on to play soccer in all divisions of college, at every level of the US National Team system, in the National Women's Soccer League, and on international professional teams.

Players they have developed have gone on to become World Cup champions, Olympians, NCAA champions, NCAA Hermann Award winners and finalists, All-Americans, Gatorade Players of the Year and finalists, United States Youth Players of the Year, United States Female Athletes of the Year, and National Women's Soccer League first-round draft picks.

They are both also winners of multiple Coach of the Year awards.

DON YAEGER is a nationally acclaimed motivational speaker, longtime associate editor of *Sports Illustrated,* and author of 25 books, nine of which have become *New York Times* best sellers. Don has written books with Hall of Fame running back Walter Payton, UCLA basketball coach John Wooden, baseball legends John Smoltz and Tug McGraw, and football stars Warrick Dunn and Michael Oher (featured in the movie *The Blind Side*), among others. He teamed with Fox News anchor Brian Kilmeade to pen the 2013 best seller *George Washington's Secret Six,* a look at the citizen spy ring that helped win the Revolutionary War, and then again in 2015 for *Thomas Jefferson and the Tripoli Pirates: The Forgotten War that Changed American History.*

Don left *Sports Illustrated* in 2008 to pursue a motivational speaking career that has allowed him to share stories learned from the greatest winners of our generation. In this capacity, he is able to share lessons from nearly three decades of studying how highly successful athletes and business professionals think, prepare, work, and live in order to consistently achieve greatness both on and off the field.

MIA HAMM became the youngest person ever to play on a U.S. national youth team at the age of 15; in 1991, when she was 19, she was the youngest person ever to play in the World Cup. She attended UNC Chapel Hill, where she helped lead the Tar Heels to four consecutive NCAA National Championships. Hamm was a member of the U.S. Women's National Soccer Team for 17 years, winning gold at the 1996 and 2004 Olympics as well as winning the 1991 and 1999 Women's World Cup.

Five years in a row she was named Soccer USA's Female Athlete of the Year (1994-1998) and she also won Soccer Player of the Year (2000, 2001, 2005) and Female Athlete of the Year (1998-2000) at the Excellence in Sports Performance Yearly Award (ESPYs). Until June 2013, she held the record for most international goals, male or female.

Hamm played for the Washington Freedom from 2001 to 2003, serves as a global ambassador for FC Barcelona, and has authored a number of books. She currently supports a variety of soccer and youth soccer organizations, as well as coaches her children's teams.

CAMILLE LEVIN played for Slammers FC in Southern California, and represented the United States on several national youth teams. She received a soccer scholarship from Stanford, where, in 2011, she assisted the game-winning goal to earn Stanford's first NCAA National Championship. She was named to the NSCAA first team All-America, NSCAA first team All-Pacific Region, first team Pac-12, and the NCAA College Cup All-Tournament Team. Following graduation, she played for the Pali Blues in the United States and then for one of Sweden's top teams, Kopparbergs/Göteborg FC. After playing a season with the Western Sydney Wanderers in Australia, Levin signed with the NWSL team, Sky Bly FC. Levin currently plays for the Orlando Pride.

KASSI MCCLUSKIE grew up playing for the elite soccer club Sereno in Scottsdale, Arizona, before receiving a scholarship to play college soccer at the University of Portland. She was a US Youth National Team member and made four NCAA playoff appearances while in college. As a highly successful coach, she led the 99G Oregon Premier League State Championship Team and Beaverton High School Varsity Girls' soccer teams. Since 2012, she has served as the Football Club Portland Elite Club National League coach.

ACKNOWLEDGMENTS

We'd like to extend a special thanks to Gary Jabara for his vision and dedication to making this book possible. He was the real force behind everything with this project.

Thank you to the legendary Mia Hamm, Camille Levin, and Kassi McCluskie, for their willingness to share their experiences as players and coaches (and, in Mia's case, as a parent, too) in order to help others navigate the process.

We are deeply appreciative of our wonderful athletes who were willing to take part in the photos for this book: Kennedy Carter, Kristen Chong, Tora Coggin, Aueree Dubach, Aaliyah Shiria Farmer, Madison Goerlinger, Julia Gomez, Abby Greubel, Faith Harper, Allison Hung, Gabi Juarez, Olivia Khoury, Kaylee Nguyen, Jenna Nighswonger, Nicholette Palomo, Arianna Presley, and Sianna Siemonsma. We are also grateful to Sean Berry for his fantastic photography, and to Jeremy Snyder and Cornerstone author Mallory Weggemann for their incredible help during the photo shoot. Thanks also to Sage Hill School and to Tarbut V'Torah Community Day School.

To all the athletes who reach out to someone who needs a little guidance, some help, a hand, a friend—you are using your sport for good and being a role model, whether you realize it or not. You inspire us.

And, finally, to all the parents who love their kids fiercely and only want to do the best thing for them, we seek to protect, to shield, to carry our children—but in doing so we can inadvertently do more harm than good. This book is for all of you who seek to aid your daughters in the best manner possible as they grow in the sport by helping them become independent and self-sufficient young women. Thank you for caring enough to do everything you do.

Join Paralympic Gold Medalist Mallory Weggemann on
your journey to becoming a Complete Athlete today!

Available Summer 2017 by downloading the Complete
Athlete app in the App store or via Google Play.
Also available in paperback at Amazon or at
www.MyCompleteAthlete.com.